You Never Said Goodbye

You Never Said Goodbye

An autobiography by
John McArdle

Copyright © 2015 John McArdle
All rights reserved.
Cover image by Sven Arnstein

ISBN: 1517180805
ISBN 13: 9781517180805
Library of Congress Control Number: 2015919421
CreateSpace Independent Publishing Platform
North Charleston, South Carolina

This book is dedicated to my mother, Edie McArdle. A woman who was widowed at the age of 38 with 5 young children. Who remarried seven years later and had another child at the age of 42, later divorcing and having to raise the children alone. She is now 87 years old and looks 67. Her children are a credit to her because of the way she brought them up, with love, care and most of all pride in all that we do.

Thank you, Mother. I love you very much.

Acknowledgments

I was travelling on a train from Preston in Lancashire to London Euston to attend a meeting for a TV series. The train was packed and it was standing room only. I got talking to a young guy and he recognised me from my TV work. I asked him what he did. He said he was a writer and that his first book had just been published, about his experience as a soldier serving in Iraq. I told him about my being brought up with an army background and about my brief spell in the Paras. Towards the end of the journey he gave me a signed copy of his book and I gave him my email address so he could keep me informed as to how the launch went.

His book was called *Squaddie: A Soldier's Story*. I read it and thought how well he could write, how it captured the life of a soldier in today's army and how interesting his story was. His name is Steven McLaughlin.

A few years later I was a guest on Radio Lancashire, talking about my life and career. When I had finished my interview I got a call from Steven; he had been listening to me on the radio and was very interested in what I'd been talking about. He said that I should write about my life, that it would make an interesting book. That planted the seeds for my writing about my story.

I kept in touch with Steven and he sent me a copy of his second book, *Clubland UK*, about his life on the nightclub doors in Blackpool. I read it and found it be another interesting and well-written book.

I started to write my own book in-between jobs, so when I wasn't acting I would write. It has taken me about three and a half years to finish. All along the way, Steven has given me help and encouragement. He is a gifted and talented writer and I am thankful for all his help along the lonely road to publication.

As my grammar was very rusty I knew was going to need the help of a good editor. I searched the internet trying to find one to no avail. Then it dawned on me that my niece, Joanna Cummings, was a proof-reader and a very good one to boot. I asked her if she would edit my book. She accepted and did a wonderful job.

Contents

Acknowledgments · vii
Prologue · xi
Wrights Terrace · 1
Another World · 7
Life Goes On · 22
Down Under · 32
The Tasman Sea · 39
Porridge · 45
Deportation · 53
Homeland · 72
My True Beginning · 83
Love of my Life · 92
More Porridge · 101
The Small Screen · 116
Brookside · 127
Henry · 158
The Place of the Dead · 166
The Duke · 177
This is My Life · 197
Selective List of Principal Performances in Theatre,
Film and Television · 205
    Theatre · 205
    Television · 206

Films · 207
Directing · 208
Awards and Accreditation · 208
About the Author · 209

Prologue

Dear Dad,

I remember the day that you left us. Not like you deserted us or anything like that, but when you left our world it was very sudden and unexpected. It was the 1st of July 1966, a lovely sunny day. I am sorry you missed the World Cup; we won it this time. You had gone off to work in Preston and Mum and the kids were at home - school holidays and all that. I remember it was a Friday because you and Mum were going to Cattrick for the weekend for some army reunion and I was looking forward to going out in the evening; being 16 it was all I could think of. I was working at the plastic ball factory in Burscough; I hated that job spraying balls all day in a confined room stinking of paint.

Then my world started to fall apart when the foreman came into the spraying room and said, "John I think you better go home - your dad's dead."

I couldn't believe what he'd just said.

"Sorry," I said, "You've made a mistake. You must mean my Grandad. My dad's too young to die."

"No," the foreman said, "it's your dad. He must have fallen off a ladder or something."

My mind was spinning like a top, all sorts of things going through my head - mostly disbelief. You were only 48, an ex -Army Physical Training instructor and fit as a butcher's dog. It couldn't be you. I wasn't crying or anything, I was just confused. I ran out of the factory and jumped on my scooter - as you know, I was a mod and loved my scooter that you and Mum had bought me for my sixteenth birthday. I didn't know where to go, too afraid to face my mother in case it was true, so I headed for our local RC church, St John's, to have a few strong words with God.

It was Friday morning, so the church was empty. I knelt in a pew and started to ask God: had he made a big mistake? It was the natural order of things for the oldest to go first, and although I loved my grandfather Tom very dearly I asked God to trade him for you. I sat in the church for a little longer trying to hold back time. What should I do next? I couldn't go home yet - it might be true. I had to avoid the truth. *I know, I'll go to Huyton in Liverpool to ask my Uncle Jack and Aunty Mary if it's true.*

I got to Huyton in a blur, and don't remember how I got there - my mind was definitely not on the road. I stopped outside my uncle's house, and I could see them rushing to the door: Uncle, Aunty, cousins, grandparents, all with the look of gloom on their faces. *My God, it's true.*

My Uncle Jack was the first to speak.
"You alright, son? Your mother's worried to death, she thinks you might have done something stupid."
"No, I thought it might be me grandad."

My grandfather had tears streaming down his face, but I was still not crying. We all piled in a couple of cars to take me home to my mother and brothers and sisters. I was dreading every part of the journey, not wanting to face reality.

We stopped outside our house. My mother was on the doorstep with some of the kids around her all in tears. This was it, it was most definitely true - I could see it in my mother's eyes. No words were said at first, we just held each other. I then broke down; it was so painful.

My mother said, "What are we going to do, son?"

What were we going to do? Losing our Dad, husband, our main man. My mother was only 38 with five children, I was 16, Sharon 11, Colleen 9 Rory 6 and Terry 4. The whole extended family was devastated. You made quite an impact on them in your life, Dad, and we were just getting to know you.

The funeral you had was really impressive with full military honours. Quite right to after all you had done for your country. The Union Jack was draped across your coffin and the pall bearers were young private soldiers from your old regiment. They fired their rifles into the air and they played the last post on bugle. What a send-off.

It was afterwards that the full impact of your loss came into effect. Mum waiting by the window for you to return from work. Your scent still on bedding and clothes, the younger kids asking where you were all the time. I know you didn't want to go, but our world was falling apart without you. It was a heart attack that finished you off, Dad, a really massive one. It was your arteries, clogged up to the hilt with all that cholesterol that you had accumulated over the years; you didn't know at the time that all that milk, butter, steak, and beer were killing you. There was nothing that could have been done. Your death was due to coronary heart disease. A hardening of the arteries. It made me start to think about the meaning of our lives – why we were here? My only thought at my age was that I had better start living my life to the full. We don't have much time on this earth.

Wrights Terrace

Let's go back a bit, Dad, to the first time I ever saw you. As you know, I was born in Sefton General Hospital, Liverpool, on the 16th of August 1949. I don't remember any of it, of course, so I don't remember seeing you. My first memories of existing is when I was about 3 years old; it was Elizabeth II's coronation day and I was dressed as a horseguard soldier, with you know, cardboard armour, helmet and sword. I've seen a photo of me and you're in the background, but I still don't remember you being there. It must have been because you were away a lot with the army. Don't worry - I'll come to the bit when I first became aware of you later.

We lived in a small terraced house in Wavertree, Liverpool. It had a parlour, a back room, where everyone listened to the radio, ate, bathed and lived. Just off was the smallest kitchen you have ever seen, with no hot water. Out the back was a yard with a toilet at the end with no electricity, so if you wanted to go at night, you went by candlelight or a torch – and by torch I mean a lighted piece of paper. And over the wall from the yard was a railway line. Upstairs in the house were two bedrooms with no electricity. At one time there were 9 people living there: my Uncle Jack and Aunty Mary, my cousins Michael and Pat, my grandma and grandad, me, my mum and sometimes you, Dad, though I can't remember that. I do remember the sleeping arrangements; my gran and grandad were in one bedroom and my cousins and I were in the other bedroom, all in the same bed. My aunty and uncle slept in the parlour and my mum slept in the back room with you, Dad, when you were home.

My grandmother was a very religious woman so there were icons and pictures all over the house of Saints and Jesus with a bleeding heart and crucifixes everywhere. We used to be so scared at bedtime because we had to go up to bed by candlelight and the shadows that fell across the room were terrifying. There used to be a picture opposite the bed of Jesus with all the little children around him and if you looked at it long enough the figures would move about in the flickering candlelight. Bedtime was something I never looked forward to.

I do remember my mum at this time; she was a beautiful dark-haired woman who loved and cared for me and who I adored. My grandma was a very stern woman who nearly always mentioned God or some Saint in every conversation. If she heard or saw something alarming she would say, *Jesus, Mary and Joseph!* or *God bless us and save us.* If my mum asked her about something she might do in the near future she would say, *If God spares me,* and if she heard something shocking she would say, *Suffering Allah.* But under all that hard religious fire shone a good heart.

It was my Grandad that I remember the most in those early days, Dad, maybe because he was around more, with you away on army duties. He was also a great character, and a wonderful story teller. Once he took me down to the Pier Head in Liverpool and we were standing at the edge of the river looking over to Birkenhead on the other side, it was beginning to go dark so all the lights from the tall buildings at Camelairds shipyard were lit.

I said, "What's that place over the water, Grandad?"
"That's New York," he replied.

I must have been about 4 years old at the time and I believed that it was New York until I was about ten.

His greatest tale was the day he told me he was John Wayne. I had just come back from seeing a John Wayne film with my mother at the local cinema. During the film I had noticed that my grandad looked a lot like him. So as soon as we got back I told him how great the film was and that he looked like John Wayne.

He then replied, "I am John Wayne."

I was so excited. I believed him without any doubt. I even told all my friends and they believed him too. He used to tell me all sorts of stories, like how he fought in the First World War. My Gran told me later that he'd got as far as Calais and hurt his leg getting on the troopship, so they sent him back home, where he spent the rest of the war. He also told me that he had been on safari in Africa and killed lions, all made up of course, but at the time I relished every word – he was my hero. I made a film about him in 1998, but I will tell you all about that later.

I loved living at Number 13, Wrights Terrace, Wavertree, Liverpool. It was a real community; everyone in the street knew one another and all the kids played safely. I think there was only one car parked there. Sadly, we had to move to Preston when I was about four. You had come back from serving abroad somewhere and we were given married quarters so we could all live together as a family. We moved to the very first place of our own in Fulwood Barracks, Preston. I was about four. I hated being away from Grandad and Granny and my cousins; they had been my extended family since I was born so it was a bit of a wrench leaving them behind. Like all kids I soon adapted to my new surroundings and got to know you a bit better, Dad. My Grandad used to send me a bar of Cadbury's chocolate in the post because he knew I loved it, and every so often they used to visit. I used to look forward to that because they used to bring me presents.

It was about this time I learned about mortality. I remember asking you if my grandparents would always be around and you told me that they would eventually die and go to Heaven. That really upset me for a while; well it still does really, knowing you are not going to live forever.

I was quite a spoilt child in terms of getting toys and treats; that is, until my sister came along. Sharon was born on the 4th of June 1954. At the time I must have been jealous because she was getting all the attention I'd had for the past five years. One day when Sharon was about eight or nine months old, she was sitting up in one of those upright classic prams and I jumped in at the opposite end. Because I was a lot heavier than a little baby, she catapulted out of the pram, landing on the floor head first. My mum and you went berserk, keeping me away from my sister for quite a long time. Living in an army barracks was brilliant for a five year-old boy with soldiers marching up and down on parade with real guns!

I can remember my first day at St Gregory's infant school. I hated leaving my mum and I think I cried all day; I was always a sensitive child. I was in class on the second day, too scared to look at the teacher so I was looking down at my desk. Then I heard her voice:

"John, would you look up please?"

So instead of looking straight ahead I looked up at the ceiling, which made all the other children in the class laugh.

"No," said the teacher, "Look up at me!"

I said, "You told me to look up and that's what I'm doing!"

By now the class was in stitches and I liked this attention. Were these the early seeds of me becoming an actor? It may have been but I think it was the school panto that clinched it.

We were doing *Ali Baba and the 40 Thieves*, and I was playing one of the thieves. We didn't have forty because that would have crowded the stage somewhat. There were about twelve of us and we had cardboard cut outs of large urns that we used to hide behind, and at a certain cue in the play we had to jump out to reveal ourselves. Well before that cue came, my cardboard urn fell down, revealing me too soon. The audience laughed and clapped. Far from being embarrassed, I was very pleased with myself, getting all this attention and only playing a small part. I later found out this was called 'upstaging', something that happened quite a lot when I later worked in Rep – but not by me, Dad., honest!

I was getting to know you more now. Sometimes you would take me into work where your job was to get soldiers fit for fighting. You were an Army Physical Training Instructor. I used to like going to the gym with you and watch you putting the squaddies through their paces. I loved the smells in there; the leather from the medicine balls and a kind of army smell – it must have been from the webbing the men wore. I felt proud watching you order the soldiers about; you were in charge and you were my dad. I started to feel secure and happy living in Fulwood Barracks – and why wouldn't I with a whole army living there to protect us?

My second sister came along two years later, Colleen, born on the 6th of April 1956. I was just getting used to Sharon getting all the attention and now I had yet another rival. Don't get me wrong, Dad: I love my brothers and sisters very much and we are a close and affectionate family, it's just when I was little I thought differently. Our stay in Fulwood Barracks was a very memorable part of my childhood. I got my first bike, a three-wheeler; I had my first accident, cutting my knee falling off my bike. Watched my first television at my friend's house (he was posh). I swallowed a bullet that I picked up from the firing range. Had my first encounter with the police, when they were making enquiries about some boys playing on a building site and stealing bricks. I admitted to playing on the site but I didn't steal any bricks.

One night you and Mum went out and left me with a babysitter. You returned about 10.30, not long after the pubs had shut. Mum's crying woke me up. I came downstairs and saw her covered in blood; you had a cut to your head and you were bleeding from your ear. I remember you comforting me and telling me not to worry, that everything was going to be alright. It was so terrifying for me seeing my parents in such a state and I couldn't stop crying. Then Mum came up to see if I was ok. She told me what a brave man you'd been defending her honour. She told me that three drunken men in the pub were looking over at her and sniggering and making rude gestures. You couldn't see this as you had your back to them. However, when you went to the toilet one of the men came over to Mum and was telling her how beautiful she was: *how about a little kiss?* Sounds like something out of a bad B movie but this was real life. When you came back this guy was still there and you told him to sling his hook or you would knock him out. This guy laughed and told you he had three mates with him.

You said, "I don't care if you've got 33 mates - if you don't move I'll move you!"

This guy sloped back to his table to confer with his buddies. You and Mum then drank up and left the pub, but as you were putting your coat on these three guys jumped on you and started to beat you up. You couldn't get your arm out of the sleeve of your overcoat to defend yourself, they were on top of you kicking and punching you. Mum went to your rescue: she took off one of her stilettos and hit one of the guys on the head with the pointed heel of her shoe. This made the man let go of you. Meanwhile you had released yourself from your overcoat and were able to defend yourself against these three thugs. You and mum got the better of them in the end and these guys ran off. I was so proud of both you and Mum for protecting one another. It was sad to see you both injured like this but it showed your courage and love for each other.

Our time in Preston was coming to an end. We were about to set off for your next posting in Hong Kong. It was September 1957 and I was eight years old.

Another World

The trip to Hong Kong in 1957 was an extremely memorable one. We got the ship from Southampton and sailed via the Suez Canal. This was the first time I had been out of the UK and I was so excited about this journey into the unknown. However for most of the journey I was seasick and this was quite a long voyage: six weeks in total. I remember sailing through the Suez Canal and most of the way it was desert either side. We would see nomads in camel trains crossing the desert.

We stopped for a few hours in Port Said and the traders in their little boats would come alongside the ship and sell their souvenirs for tourists, hoisting them up on a rope to you. If you decided you would like to do a deal you would send the money back down to them. Young Arab boys of my age would swim alongside the ship, wanting you to throw coins into the water so they could dive for them. Even though I was sick most of the trip, I still loved being on the ship. We saw and experienced so much. Some days we would see flying fish, and sometimes dolphins would follow the ship for a while. The most awesome sight I saw was a pod of gigantic humpback whales, spouts of water coming from their blowholes and their huge tails flipping out of the water when they dived.

Crossing the Equator was also something that stuck in my mind, the crew and the soldiers were all in fancy dress and played silly games, throwing water over each other and performing other rituals and silly things that are linked to crossing the Equator. I got very sunburned on that day; I had huge blisters on my back and shoulders. There was no proper sun protection in those days. I think they used baby oil or something similar.

I remember that we stopped in Colombo, the capital of Sri Lanka, and I begged you to let me go ashore with a family that we had become friends with on board. They had children my age and I wanted to go with them when they went ashore to visit the city. You and Mum eventually let me go after instructions from mum not to stray from my friend's family; little did you know that day you'd almost lose me.

After visiting the city, the family decided to go to the local beach. We had our swimming costumes and towels with us, as this was pre-arranged. I thought it would just be a bit of a paddle and a splash about like we did at New Brighton but the sea here was much wilder and huge waves crashed right onto the shore. My friend's mother asked me if I could swim and not wanting to seem like a baby, I told them I could. The family swum out into deeper water and said I should swim out to them, so I kept my feet on the sand and pretended to swim by moving my arms in a breast stroke fashion. Suddenly the sea bed dropped away and I couldn't touch the ground with my feet anymore. At the same time a massive wave dumped on top of me and pushed me under the water. I was gasping for breath and disoriented and I didn't know which way was the surface.

All of a sudden the father of the family grabbed me out of the water and carried me to the shore. I thought I was dying. I had swallowed loads of sea water and couldn't get my breath. I was crying and wanted my mum so they took me back on board and told you and Mum what had happened. The first thing you decided to do when we got to Hong Kong was to teach me to swim.

Although I had been sad to leave England I remember the excitement of arriving in Hong Kong after that long trip by sea. Being on dry land after all that time took a bit of adjustment. I had just begun to get used to the motion of the ship and now still for too long made me feel a bit unsteady and sick so I was unlucky on both counts! The first impression I got from Hong Kong was the heat and the smells, a mixture of cooking and drains. We were driven from the port to the outskirts of the city, to a hotel called the Tiger Bay. The first night in that hotel is still etched in my memory.

You and mum were going down to dinner, all dressed up in your finery. Because I was the eldest you told me to look after my younger sisters while you were having dinner in the hotel. Mum was a bit worried about leaving us after all she was only 28, and had never been out of Liverpool – now she was in the Far East in this strange land. You told her not to worry, that one of the hotel staff would look in on us, and anyway you were just down the hall. Well, Sharon, Colleen and I were in your double bed with a huge mosquito net covering us and we were scared to death.

After a while my sisters dropped off to sleep. I was wide awake, watching the mosquito net suddenly come alive with creatures I had never seen before in my life – except maybe in the zoo or nature books. First came the mosquitoes, of course, followed by some small lizards, then some small spiders, then more of the same only bigger. I was petrified. I decided to share my horror with my sisters, so I woke them up. Their screams, I'm sure, could be heard back in Liverpool. Then I joined in with them because I'd noticed a hole in the net.

The door to the room suddenly swung open, and three or four Chinese faces were staring down at us, which made us worse – we thought they had come to kill us. Then you and mum appeared, napkin still tucked in your shirt, knives and forks in your hands. That was it – the cavalry had arrived, and we were consoled. You didn't eat that night.

After a few days in the hotel, we got used to the insects, lizards and the new aromas. Our first impressions of the Chinese staff could not have been more wrong, they were the nicest people you could want to meet. They made a huge fuss of us; called me *Master* and the girls *Misses*, and were so amazed at how pale we were. As for Colleen's red hair, they just wanted to touch it all the time. They loved children and all our fears about being in this strange place disappeared. We were due to stay in the Tiger Bay Hotel for two or three weeks until our Army living quarters were ready. Mum must have thought her dreams had come true. I don't think she had been on a proper holiday before and here she was, in a luxury hotel in an exotic country, being waited on hand and foot.

On the last week of our stay, the girls and I were playing in the hotel gardens. We noticed in the far distance beyond the bay that the sky was almost black and dark clouds were on the move towards us at a fast pace. Some of the hotel staff came running out and grabbed our hands and told us to quickly get back into the hotel. We were ushered up to our rooms. Mum was up there but I think you were at the barracks or somewhere. I had seen storms at home in England but nothing like what we were about to witness. That black sky we saw was now above our hotel, along with a torrential downpour and the strongest winds I have ever experienced. The palm trees in the gardens were almost bent double and debris was flying everywhere; we could hear glass breaking and doors slamming – the noise was deafening. Once again we were scared to death. One of the lovely staff members came to tell us to stay in our rooms and not to worry: that this happened every year and it would subside in four or five hours. It was our first monsoon and it lasted through the night. The next morning, we went outside to see the damage and it was like a bomb had been dropped on the place. Palm trees felled, plants uprooted, most of the windows in the hotel smashed. We even saw some of the hotel staff bicycles mangled and up in the trees. Unbelievably, no one was hurt. A few days later we were leaving for our new home on the mainland. It was sad to leave because we liked the staff so much; but they came out of the building to wave us off on our next adventure.

We were heading to our new home on the mainland side of Hong Kong. We travelled in an Army staff car and headed down the hill into the city, Victoria; from there we got the ferry to Kowloon, the second largest city in Hong Kong. The whole place was so densely populated and so busy, large numbers of sampans and junks in the harbour all trading and selling. I remember you telling me at the time that whole families lived on these boats, sometimes not coming ashore for months at a time; everything was done from these small vessels including their ablutions. It seemed unbelievable to me. It took us about an hour or so to get out of the city and onto the country roads. We passed lots of farms and miles and miles of paddy fields with lots of people young and old – including women with babies on their backs – picking the rice crops. We then started to drive up a very winding road on the Tai Mo Shan Mountain, which went on for miles. I was feeling very car sick (I was quite a sickly child!) and we had to stop a few times so I could get out the car and take some fresh air – and it was lovely fresh air in the mountain compared to the humidity further down. After about two hours we started to descend into a valley.

Arriving in Sek Kong village at around midnight, we were dropped off at a small bungalow with a veranda, which was to be our home for the next year. I had my own bedroom, my sisters shared and you had the main bedroom. It was a completely new way of life for us with mosquito nets over the beds and ceiling fans in every room. The next morning, we awoke to bright sunshine and someone was in the kitchen making breakfast but it wasn't you or Mum. I went into the kitchen and there was this middle aged Chinese woman buttering toast.

"Good morning, Master," she said. "My name is Ah Yen. I am your Amah Would you like cornflakes or toast or both?"

You explained later that Ah Yen was our maid and that she would be living with us in a small room attached to the house. She was to do all the chores: washing, ironing, cooking. Babysitting in fact anything domestic. The Army paid her; this was to create employment for the indigenous people. Mum could not handle this at first as she was used to doing everything herself; she was from a working class Liverpool family and this was far from anything she had ever experienced. We soon got used to having a maid, although my mum used to feel so guilty that she used to help Ah Yen with the housework. But Ah Yen would say,

"No Missy, this is my job. Please – you don't have to help me."

So Ah Yen did everything but the Sunday roast. We became such good friends with her that she was like a member of the family.

After a few months we settled in and enjoyed this new colonial lifestyle. My sisters and I went to school from 8.30 am to 1.30 then went swimming (thanks for teaching me, Dad). Mum used to meet up with the other sergeants' wives for coffee mornings and afternoon tea which was very civilised. I remember every Sunday you would get up before Mum and make us all a cooked breakfast, then you would take us to the NAFFI and buy us sweets, before going off to the sergeants' mess while Mum cooked the Sunday lunch.

One particular Sunday the dinner was almost ready and there was no sign of you, so mum told me to go and get you from the mess, which was about a quarter of a mile away. I went to the reception at the mess and asked for you, and the soldier on duty told me I could go in and get you. You were at the bar with your mates, absolutely pissed.

"What are you doing here?" you said.
"Your dinner's ready," I said.

There was lots of banter going on with your mates. They called you Mac – that was the first time I had heard anyone call you that apart from Mum. You were finishing your beer and your mates bought me crisps and a shandy, rubbing my head and saying things like, *Don't join the Army when you grow up, son,* and *Get your dad home before your mum comes up and drags him by the short and curlies.* Eventually I got you out of the mess but you were all over the place, staggering and swearing at any Chinese people that looked at you. It was really embarrassing. At one point you lay down in the middle of the road and the traffic had to go around you. I got you up and headed home. On the way we had to cross a small stream and you decided to sit in it and fill your pockets with lots of small frogs that were in the water.

You kept on saying, "Shush, don't tell your mum about the frogs."

We got through the front door. Mum was really annoyed to say the least and said you would have to wait for your dinner to be warmed up as it had gone cold. When Mum went into the kitchen you started to get the frogs out of your pocket and place them all around the living room. When Mum came in with your dried-up dinner she didn't notice all these frogs in her living room at first. Then she caught sight of one, then two and started to scream the house down when she saw them all hopping all over the place. I think your dinner ended up on your head.

I recall one time when you and Mum where on the veranda having a drink and Mum asked me to go into your bedroom and get a magazine. I went looking for this magazine and was rooting around in the bedside cabinet on your side, Dad and I came across a handgun. I picked it up – it was so heavy – and started to point it at objects and pretend to shoot them. Then you came in grabbed the gun off me and swiped me across the head. You went ballistic, saying I could have killed myself or someone else. I wondered why you kept it in your bedside cabinet. At the time it was still the Cold War; there was always some sort of threat from either Russia or China and the Chinese border was only about ten miles from where we lived. Mum told me later that in the event of the Chinese overrunning our base, he would first use the gun on Mum and then us kids so we would not run into the hands of the murdering Chinese army! Thank God they decided not to invade us and that you were never put into that situation. I wonder whether you would ever have been able to do it.

My brother Rory was born while we lived in Sek Kong village. It was the 5th of January 1959. Mum said you got drunk, and then told her you'd registered his birth with the Chinese authorities so he would be liable for National Service in the Chinese Army when he reached the age of 18. Mum was worried for quite a while until you eventually told her it was a joke. It's no wonder you were always getting hit with flying objects.

Ah Yen used to look after Rory when he was a baby; she also had a baby of her own, Ah Ying. The Army said you had to dismiss the Amah if they had children, but you kept her on because she was a loyal worker and we had got so close to her. You never let the Army know about her baby which I think was very thoughtful of you Dad because it meant she didn't lose her income. So when Ah Yen looked after Rory she would put him in the playpen with her son, Ah Ying, whilst she got on with her work. After a while Rory began to pick up some Chinese as he was spending so much time with Ah Ying. That's the best way to learn a language – but unfortunately Rory did not remember a word of Chinese when he came back to England two years later.

We lived in Sek Kong Village for a year and then moved to Stanley Fort on Hong Kong Island. This was a larger Army base and not as nice as Sek Kong Village. The Army quarters were a block of flats, and we lived on the third floor with no garden, so we had to make do with the playing field where the soldiers trained. We got used to the new surroundings and I made some new friends. One friend in particular was a very bad influence indeed: Ian Bunting.

One morning Ian called for me to get the bus to school. As we walked to the bus stop he said it was his birthday and he had lots of birthday money and we should take the day off school and have some fun with it. Well I was easily led into temptation and said, *Let's do it*. So we missed the school bus, then cadged a lift off one of the soldiers going into Victoria, Hong Kong's capital. We told this man we had missed the school bus, so he had no idea we were bunking off school for the day. We arrived in Victoria at about 9.30am. The city was so busy at that time in the morning and we went into the main market place where they sold absolutely everything, food, electrical goods, toys, clothes, if they could sell it they sold it. Ian got out his birthday money, wads of dollars, and so the spending spree began. I had never seen so much money in my life.

He said, "Get what you like – I'll pay for it."

We bought cigarettes, flick knifes, stick-on tattoos and lots of sweets and Chinese fireworks, mainly bangers or firecrackers as they called them.

The Chinese were totally amused by these two 11 year-old boys smoking fags and letting off bangers. When it got to lunchtime we went looking for somewhere to eat. We came across this bar/café, so we went inside. It was packed on this Friday lunchtime, with British and American military and some very attractive Chinese girls. A pretty Chinese girl came and asked us what we wanted.

"Chips and ice cream," we said.
"Ok," she said, "and would you like some girls to sit with you?"
"Fine," I said, "Ian has lots of money, he can buy them lunch."

The soldiers and sailors were killing themselves laughing and the pretty Chinese girls were making a fuss of us. Little did we know at the time: we were in a brothel. We had our lunch and left and we could still hear them laughing half way down the street.

Next we caught the ferry to Kowloon to have a look round there. After buying more useless things in the markets we decided to go to the cinema. It was late afternoon by now and the bus back from the school had gone, but we decided we would watch the film and then get a taxi home. We were the only Westerners in the Chinese cinema so everyone was looking at us especially as the film was called 'Adam and Eve', and as you can guess it was a bit rude for a couple of kids. We didn't understand a word that was said but I think we got the gist. By the time the film had finished it was about 7.30 in the evening and we realised we had lost all track of time.

Back at home, however, there was a major search going on for two missing boys. The Hong Kong police, the Military Police and the whole of your Regiment were part of the search. Of course we had no idea but thought because it was dark by now perhaps we ought to get back home. We started to get a bit worried because Hong Kong was such a densely populated city and at night it seemed even worse. Because it was a Friday night trying to get a taxi was difficult so we decided to get a bus. Our pockets were stuffed with sweets, toys, bangers, comics and lots of dollars left from Ian's birthday money.

Suddenly we saw a Military Police Land Rover coming towards us. Ian started to panic and was giving his money and gifts to the people waiting at the bus stop with us. He told me to do the same. I thought he was mad but he grabbed the stuff off me and gave it to the strangers. The Land Rover pulled up and two Military Policemen got out.

"Are you John McArdle and Ian Bunting?"
"Yes," I said.
"Well you better get in the Land Rover - the whole world has been looking for you."

When we arrived back at the barracks there was a large party waiting for us. You were all dressed in evening wear as there was a Regimental Ball that night. I remember Mum was crying, so pleased that I'd been found and was alright, but you were angry for all the worry and trouble I had caused and I knew I was in for it later. The next day I found out that the money Ian had got was stolen from his mother's purse – over 500 dollars. I had to pay some of it back out of my pocket money even though I didn't know it was stolen but that was only one of the incidents I got into with Ian – more to come later.

During the school holidays in Hong Kong we had so much time on our hands. We either went to the beach with our mum and her friends or just played around the barracks pretending to be soldiers fighting the Japanese. This was because the barracks we lived in, Stanley Fort, had been occupied by the Japanese during the Second World War. We would sometimes find relics left behind by the Japanese Army, a bayonet or an old helmet or even part of a rifle. Our imaginations would run wild about what happened during the war: we heard stories of torture and British people being beheaded and nuns being thrown to the sharks. You can imagine what was going through the minds of ten year old boys – we thought it was great. Sometimes we would stray outside the camp and come across a gang of Chinese boys of about our age. We would swap stuff with them: toys for cigarettes, English comics for Chinese ones; anything that was different we wanted. Sometimes we would have stone fights, very dangerous when I look back, hurling huge rocks at one another. The game would stop when someone got a nasty gash.

One day the dreaded Ian Bunting and I went on another adventure outside the barracks into the countryside. We took some pop and sweets with us because we were exploring and we thought we may be some time. Walking up a hillside, we came upon a huge area covered in huge pots with joss sticks and photos of people around them. Ian and I were curious as to what was in the pots, so Ian took the lid off one and pulled out a human skull. *Wow, what a find, real human bones.* Then Ian dared me to take the lid off the next one but I was a little scared – not of the bones, but because I thought there might be a snake in there. Ian pushed me out of the way and began pulling all the bones out of the pot. The contents of the jar lay all around us.

"What shall we do now?" I said.
"Put them in order," said Ian, so we started to assemble this jigsaw of bones.

Our biology teacher would have been proud of us. Five minutes later we had a full skeleton and we sat there looking at it, discussing whether it was male or female, young or old? What they could have died of etc like proper little anthropologists. While we were sitting there admiring our handy work, we heard shouting just below us, and looked to see about five angry Chinese people running towards us. We ran like hell and didn't stop until we reached the safety of the camp. We thought we would hear no more about it, but how wrong we were.

The local Chinese community leader made a complaint to the Commanding Officer at the base. In the eyes of the Chinese, we had taken someone's ancestor out of their resting place and exposed their remains to the evil spirits and the world. The Commanding Officer of the Regiment lined up all the ten to twelve year-olds for an identity parade. The old man walked along the line but failed to pick anyone out, thank God. He must have thought we all looked the same. Now I wish to apologise to any of those relatives that I may have offended.

Well, Dad, we spent three eventful and happy years in Hong Kong thanks to you and your profession. It opened my mind to the world, and educated me more than my schooling; I lived close to people from a completely different race and religion to my own. The Chinese people, I found, were clever, kind and open. Our Amah, Ah Yen, even learned English with a Scouse accent. In fact it was hard saying goodbye to her as she had become part of the family.

So we were to return to the UK, my very first time on an aircraft. The year was 1960 and the trip home in the plane was quite memorable. We landed in Istanbul to refuel before our final leg to Heathrow. As we were taking off, I and a number of the passengers noticed that one of the engines was on fire.

I think I casually said to you, "Dad, look the plane's burning…"

Next thing you were shouting to one of the Air Hostesses and the message was relayed to the pilot and the take-off was aborted. So we were stranded in the airport for about ten hours while they replaced our flight. It must have been a bit of a nightmare for you and mum, with four kids to keep occupied.

It was great being back in England, seeing my grandparents and cousins again after such a long time. Our next posting was the Isle of Wight. As you know, our camp was right next to one of the most high profile prisons in the United Kingdom, HMP Parkhurst. You would scare us, saying that the most notorious criminals were imprisoned there and they were always trying to escape. We were so nervous for the first few months that a crazed killer was going to stab us on the way to school. Thanks, Dad!

Our youngest brother Terry was born here on the 16th of September 1960. We were only posted on the island for about twelve months but it seemed like three years; it was as if time stood still. Your story of escaping prisoners came true – one of the high-risk prisoners did escape and we had to stay in for a few days until he was caught.

Next you were posted to Crownhill Barracks in Plymouth, another school to get used to, another accent to imitate, another place to fit in. This was such good grounding for my acting I suppose, learning to adapt to all these different environments. Well, Dad, after Plymouth, as you will remember, we headed back north to Bourscough, Lancashire, which was to be your last posting before your retirement from the Army. I was a big boy now, thirteen and we settled in well to our new surroundings. I must admit the saying is true: people do seem friendlier in the North.

After a year, we moved out of our Army house and into civilian life. The council gave you a house on a new estate, a brand new semi-detached with fields at the back. You loved it. You had your Army pension, you were about to start your own cleaning company and you were only 46. We were all happy there. I went to St Bede's Secondary Modern in Ormskirk and that's when I found out you had another family from a previous marriage.

I remember going into school one day and looking at the roll of honour and noticed the name Angela McArdle on it. Because I thought McArdle was an unusual name I told you about it. You said quite casually, "That's probably your stepsister."

You then told me the whole story about you being a young sergeant in India, meeting your first wife and having two children, Angela and Chris. Then coming back to England and getting a divorce.

You had this whole other life before us. I couldn't get my head around it. Why didn't you tell us about this before? If I hadn't gone to St Bede's at that particular time, would you have told me? It turns out that you got married in India when you were a young Sergeant stationed out there during the war. The woman you married was above your class by the sounds of it, the daughter of some high-ranking British official in India. You had two children with her, then returned to England after the war and divorced soon after. I met up with Chris and Sheila not long after you died and they filled me in on your early history.

Born in Liverpool in 1917, the eldest of five children. Your parents were Irish Catholics and were very poor indeed. You went to school with no shoes on your feet and would go down to the fish market to collect scraps for your evening meal. When you reached the age of 17 you joined the Army, where you got three meals a day, clothing, a roof over your head and a good pair of boots. You joined the Army out of necessity not loyalty and it turned out to be the best thing you did. You made a good career out of it.

I must say, going to St Bede's was a bit of a turning point in my young life. Although I was an average student and didn't like school that much, I did enjoy my English class with Mr Mason; we called him Meatball Mason because of his size. He was an excellent teacher. He brought the English lesson alive by getting us up on our feet and acting out scenes from the books we were studying. It was fun and I enjoyed every minute of it. Mr Mason encouraged me to join the school drama group. I did join and one of my first parts was playing the lead in a period drama, my character was a British Army officer in the Crimean war.

The play was a success and I got great feedback from my fellow students and the teachers. Before this play most of the teachers didn't know my name, now they were all coming up to me saying, *Well done the other night, McArdle*. This was my first taste of fame on a small scale. Well when

I did eventually leave school at fifteen my thoughts were not for the stage, however – I thought you had to be posh to go into acting. Although I had no idea what I wanted to do when I left school, I still felt excited about life. We lived in a nice home on the outskirts of a large village, you and mum were still relatively young, I had lovely brothers and sisters. Life was good.

Then two years later, at the age of 48, you were taken from us. The rest of this letter is what has been happening to me since that day.

Life Goes On

Let's get back to just after you left us for good.

If you remember you had just started an industrial cleaning business and it was just starting to take off. In fact soon after you died we found out you had won a cleaning contract for Fulwood Barracks in Preston.

You left so much behind for my poor grieving mum to sort out. She was in quite a state about you going for a very long time. She listened to family members about what to do with your car and business and I think she was badly advised in hindsight. But at the time she didn't care, her mind was elsewhere, she was grieving and had five children to look after. I still couldn't believe you had gone and this was the start of my quest to grab as much out of life as I could, some of it would be great and fantastic and some would be a little dark and scary. Life after you was trying to get back to some kind of normality, although it would take a very long time for that to happen.

I left the ball factory and found some other unskilled work in Ormskirk, very convenient because that's where my mates lived and where we used to hang out. So my life at 17 consisted of working all day and going out nearly every night of the week. I was a mod, so clothes and music were very important to me. I had two close friends Tabby and Picky and we were the top mods in this little market town in Lancashire. We were not just in the 'In Crowd' – we *were* the In Crowd.

Along with the style and the music came the girls and the drugs. Makes us sound a bit like pop stars. The music we liked was not your Beatles or your Stones, it was soul music, rhythm and blues, jazz, and this was before Northern Soul. We went to all-nighters, like The Room at the top in Wigan, the Twisted Wheel in Manchester and the Burnley Cavern. We never drank much in those days. It was a couple of pints at the start of the night, then it was pills, amphetamines. Blueys, Black Bombers, Deprozel. You felt fantastic for seven or eight hours then you felt ill for the rest of the day – it wasn't worth it really because you had very bad comedowns.

I had just started this lifestyle while you were still with us, but you didn't notice. I think you thought that I was just a bit weird. I think in your time teenagers worked on the docks or joined the army like yourself, all this freedom of self-expression and all that were alien to you. I had my first real sexual experience at 16 with an older woman of 17! After a few months with her I thought I was Casanova and couldn't wait to date every girl in the world. I started to think what I was going to do with my life: I didn't want to be working in dead-end jobs and I wanted to see the world again and have a more interesting life. So I was about to make a huge decision but one that I later regretted.

I mulled over in my mind what I needed to do to change my life. My first thought was the Merchant Navy but I get really bad seasickness even on the Mersey Ferry, so that was ruled out. I couldn't afford to move to London. I had no option other than to do something that seemed natural: join the Army. But which regiment? There could be only one choice: the regiment that made you what you were. The parachute regiment. One of Britain's elite forces.

This is one of the toughest experiences I have ever had. I went along to the Army Recruitment office on London Road in Liverpool. The sergeant giving me my interview was trying to put me off joining the Paras, saying I would benefit from joining an Infantry Regiment first then doing

'P Company' for my Para wings at a later stage. I would have none of this, it was Paras or nothing. So after turning down his good advice I went ahead with the application, which consisted of a written test, basic English and Maths and the physical that was to be held in Aldershot. I travelled to Aldershot to do the next part of my test, to gain acceptance to join the Parachute Regiment. Arriving at Maida Barracks I was greeted by a young private who directed me to the guardhouse where I met my first NCO, a corporal. The greeting from the corporal was very basic.

"Drop your shit there, get into those fatigues, stick on that helmet and follow me."

He led me and a group of lads of different ages and backgrounds to the assault course. This assault course consisted of various apparatus, rope ladders, walls, scrabbling nets and ditches with barbed wire suspended very low, which you had to crawl under. Standing around watching were a group of officers from different armies from around the world: Greek, American, and Italian. They had come to observe how the British Parachute Regiment select their recruits.

The corporal told us to take a walk around the course and familiarise ourselves with what we were about to tackle. He then informed us that we had to complete the course three times in five minutes to be selected for the Paras. We got into a line, about fifteen of us, and the corporal blew his whistle. The first obstacle was pretty easy – you just ran up a plank and jumped into a ditch on the other side. The next bit was not so easy. You had to scale a wall of about eight feet high which meant taking a running jump to reach it and then haul yourself up and jump down the other side. My heart was racing at this point, partly because of the adrenalin and part because of the physical exertion. Next came the scrambling net. This was shaped like the letter A, and you climbed up and then over the other side. This was very tricky because if you didn't put your feet in the right place you would lose your balance and fall through the net. One bloke put his foot through one of the holes in the net, fell backwards and was left dangling. Once over this you ran up a small ramp about twelve inches wide, six feet off the ground and about 20 feet long and sloped down the other side. This was difficult because you had to run fast and keep your balance on the very thin plank. Next you dropped down and had to crawl through a very small tunnel, 25 feet long and filled with six inches of water. As you came out of this stinking tunnel you were smacked on the helmet with a pick axe handle by the corporal, which he said simulated an explosion. You then had to sprint 100 yards, jump over a ditch and then do the course another two times. I managed to qualify even though I suffer with asthma. I am afraid, Dad, that you were the cause of it. You didn't know, though, so I shall tell you.

It was a Sunday morning, and I was about five years old. Mum had got up to make the bacon and eggs and I was jumping on you in bed; we were messing about like father and son do. I crawled under the covers and you trapped me with your legs and I couldn't get out. I started to panic because I was having difficulty breathing and the dust from the blanket was making me choke. I screamed for you to let me out but you just trapped me tighter. By now I was in a state, I never knew about death but this was close to it. Mum came in and saved me. She shouted at you to let me go, she got me out and started shouting at you, saying how stupid you were and that I was just a boy and you were too rough. I don't know why you did this –were you trying to toughen me up or were you just playing? So I am afraid, Dad, you were responsible for me having asthma and claustrophobia. I still have it to this day, although I like to think I have it under control.

The training for the Paras was really tough; it was constant physical training every single day. I was in a dorm with about fifteen other recruits. They woke you up at 6am and you got into your shorts and t-shirt and went for a three-mile run. You then showered and shaved. Then you had breakfast, you returned to your barrack room and stripped your bed, folding the sheets and blankets into this neatly stacked sandwich at the bottom of your bed. You then had to open your locker to be inspected. Everything had to be on display at a certain angle. It was a bit liked having obsessive compulsive disorder forced on you. Your uniform had to be neatly ironed and spotlessly cleaned and your boots had to shine like glass. It was then time for kit inspection; a horrible Corporal by the name of Moriarty would walk along the line inspecting your bedding and kit and no matter how good your stuff was, he would find something wrong. If you were unfortunate enough to have a toothbrush or a razor a millimetre out of line you were put on show parade. Show parade meant you had to take whatever he pulled you up on – say your bed roll if it was untidy – and take it up to the guard room at 6pm to have it inspected again. If there was anything wrong with it a second time you were put on a charge. I remember once my whole wardrobe was picked out to be taken up to the guard room, which was about a quarter of a mile from the dorm, so I had to get a mate to help me carry it up there. After room inspection it was drill parade, which consisted of marching in formation. Luckily I had been in the Army Cadets for three years so it was easy for me but watching the others trying to coordinate their arms and legs going off in different directions meant I was always getting shouted at for laughing at them. The NCOs that took you for drill would shout out constant insults in an aggressive way, usually very crude but sometimes amusing, like *McArdle! Open your legs wider; your balls are in a little bag, they won't fall out.* That was one of the milder ones.

You would march around for about an hour then it would be personnel inspection. The NCO would walk along the line looking at your uniform and putting his face very close to yours looking to see if you had shaved close enough or your hair was short enough, if your cap badge was in the right place: two inches above the left eye. If anything was out of place it meant show parade. Sometimes they would tell you to change into fatigues, and you would come out at the double. If one person was late you had to go back in and change into what you had on before. This would go on until everyone was on parade in time. Late morning you would do some classroom battle tactics, which came under the heading of military education. At 1pm it would be lunch in the canteen, a time to catch up with your mates and bitch about the NCOs. After lunch it would be the Trainasium. This was an assault course fifty feet off the ground, so if you made a mistake on this it was broken bones or worse. After you came off the Trainasium you would go for a run along the tank tracks for about three miles. Outside your barrack room after the run you would finish off with 100 press-ups and 100 sit-ups. Then it was a shower and teatime, and after tea it was show parade if you had been unlucky. The rest of the evening, what was left of it, you spent in the dorm cleaning your kit and getting ready for the next day.

I'm telling you all this, Dad, but you know it already. You had been one of these instructors and I know you'd had been just as tough.

I became more disillusioned about the Army every day, maybe because I spent most of my life attached to it because it was your career and we lived in army barracks. I don't think I could have killed anyone; I liked the training and the playing at soldiers but when it came to the reality: no thank you. So after two months I left, although if you had still been around I think I would have stayed in, out of fear. Although I do remember asking you one day if I should join the Army or not, and you left it to me to decide. You told me that you had had no choice to do anything else at the time, that it was about survival for you. You said it was up to me and you never influenced me to become a soldier just because you were. It's a lesson I've learnt from you, not to force your children into doing something because *you* want them to.

After leaving the army I returned home to Liverpool, back with Mum and the kids. I soon got back into my old ways, staying out all night, taking amphetamines and going to the Twisted Wheel in Manchester or the Blackpool Mecca club. My two best mates had jobs with some sort of future. Picky was on an apprenticeship and Tabby was at college. I just took any job that was easy and good money. Our social life started on a Friday night: meet at the Fox and Goose in Southport, score some drugs, have a few pints and pick up some girls. It ended on a Sunday night. It was a limited hedonistic lifestyle, limited because financially I couldn't do everything I wanted. I was in and out of jobs all the time; at this point in the 60s you could leave a job on the Friday and start a new one on the Monday. I did everything from trainee manager at a local supermarket to a job in a wood yard, from a lab worker in a photo developing firm to a second man on a lorry. But the best paid job was on a building site. It was hard dirty work in all weathers, but the money was good for unskilled work. So this was my life, Dad, work hard, play hard with no ambition or regard for my future. My poor mother was not yet forty and she had to raise four other kids under the age of ten alongside the worry of me and my reckless lifestyle. One particular night I remember being in possession of quite a lot of amphetamines and was selling them to pay for my own stash. This next part I will have to rely on from what other people told me, because I only remember coming round. Apparently I was not having much luck selling my stuff so I started popping more into my own mouth: because the drug was taking a long time to take effect I must have thought they were weak and needed to top up. My friends said that I was staggering all over the place and they thought I might be drunk. We went to a party at someone's house and I was throwing up and frothing at the mouth, so a couple of my friends decided to take me to Casualty. I found out 40 years later it was my friends Picky and Tabby that took me to casualty that night and saved my life.

They placed me in the waiting area and left because the police would be involved and they didn't want to be implicated. I came round on a gurney and the medical staff were pushing a tube down my throat to pump my stomach. I passed out again and came round on a ward hearing all the moans and groans of the sick and suffering people around me. This made me paranoid and I started screaming for help. A nurse came rushing over and calmed me down. In the morning I had a visit from the police, the drug squad. I told them that someone I didn't know had maybe slipped something into my drink. Likely story they thought, but what could they do? Later on my cousin, Pat and her husband, Jimmy came to collect me to take me home to face my poor Mum.

When we arrived home not only my mother was waiting for me but the whole family, uncles, aunties and grandparents. I felt so ashamed; they were so good about it, trying to help, saying it was a reaction to your death. I said I would change my friends and keep away from drugs. I didn't keep my promise – the very next day I was back with the same friends and doing the same things.

Why was I taking so many drugs and almost killing myself? Was it because of your death? Who knows - but that brush with death didn't deter me.

I am 18 now, Dad, still doing unskilled work. I worked for your younger brother, Frank for a while as a roofer, so I suppose you could class that as semi-skilled. I was still trying to live the hedonistic lifestyle on a small wage. One thing in my favour – I wasn't lazy, and I did work hard. When I turned 19 I realised I was soon be turning twenty and that seemed old, so my next plan was to get out of the mundane 9 to 5 and seek some adventure. But where and how?

Travel was foremost in my mind but that would cost money. Again I thought about joining the Merchant Navy, getting paid to travel to lots of exotic countries. Then I remembered how seasick I was travelling to Hong Kong, so that idea bit the dust. I got talking to some guy in a pub who told me that his brother had emigrated to Australia for £10 but this was going to be scrapped in 1970. It was now 1969, so if I wanted to take this offer up I had to act fast. I made enquires at the Australian Embassy and they sent me the forms to apply. I told all my mates about this latest plan and they thought I was mad.

"It's a backward country," they said, "behind the times in fashion and music and it's the other side of the world. Why would you want to go there?"

"Well it's cheap to get there and the weather's so much better than here and I might make my fortune there."

That was it – I had made my mind up. I filled the forms in and sent them off. I passed all the medicals. They needed roof tilers out there, so – I was going.

I told my mum about my plan and she just thought it was just one of my hair-brained schemes. She didn't think I was serious. Meanwhile I got a job in Ford's because the money was good for doing shift work. Most of the guys in Ford's were decent blokes, but this was going to be their lives for the next thirty odd years or so. I knew I would only be there for six months and then I could get away from this drug culture I was involved in because one day it was going to kill me. One of my good friends, Loz decided he wanted to follow me out to Australia so he applied to emigrate too. I worked hard for that six months, doing as many shifts as I could and trying not to go out too much.

When I started to buy things for my trip – new suitcase, summer clothes and so on, my mother realised I was serious.

She said, "You know its 13,000 miles away. You can't come home at the weekends, you know that, and I will be worried sick."

I know I was selfish but your death made me realise how short life was.

I said, "Look, Mum, if you really don't want me to go I won't."
She said, "You do what you have to do. You're my eldest son and although I will miss you so much and worry all the time, I don't want to stand in your way'.

This was the night before I was leaving and I was feeling sad, scared and guilty that I was leaving my mother with four children not long after she had lost you.
She had worked so hard to keep our family together and I was leaving her. But I had to go ahead now; it was too late to turn back. The next

morning was the worst, just before the taxi came to take me to the station, my brothers and sisters came in to say goodbye to me and it broke my heart. I shall never forget it, they were all crying, begging me not to leave them, even my sister Colleen, who I used to fight and argue with, was distraught. Then the taxi arrived and my mum clung to me for what seemed like forever. Getting into that taxi was the hardest thing I have ever had to do.

Down Under

The journey was a long one, with only two landings before Sydney: Munich, which I don't remember and Rangoon which I very much do. We landed there at about midnight. We walked from the plane to the terminal, which resembled a big wooden hut, and there was bamboo scaffolding around the building as there was some repair work going on. The terminal building itself consisted of a bar, a small office and some tables. Sitting at the tables were some local people and what looked like ex-pats from a Graham Greene novel dressed in crumpled linen suits, unshaven and dishevelled. To me this was what travel was all about, meeting people like this, exotic and interesting and somewhat eccentric.

Getting off the plane at Sydney was so exciting, with my whole life in front of me I felt great. The heat and humidity were so intense it felt like you were wrapped in a sauna. People from the immigration department met me; they welcomed me to Australia and gave me accommodation in a migrant's hostel for two weeks, by which time you had to find a job and your own accommodation.

In those two weeks I made some new friends and settled in to this new and very different way of life from the one I had been used to. It was September 1969, and the spring weather was still quite hot, so people were walking around in t-shirts and shorts and the sun shone almost every day. During the two weeks at the hostel I found a job in an engineering factory and some temporary accommodation in a boarding house. The job was awful, noisy, smelly, boring and low pay, but what else could I do with no qualifications? The boarding house was awful too; I shared a room with about six other blokes, all older than me. Sometimes I would be woken in the middle of the night when one of the guys came in drunk, shouting and swearing at everyone. They would call me a Pommy bastard and tell me to *fuck off back to my own country*. They were very welcoming. I had to get out of this place soon, but I was waiting for my friend Loz to join me so we would get a flat together. I waited two months but no word from my friend. There was no Internet or Skype then, and it took about 3 weeks before you got a letter. It was only by chance that I found out Loz was in Sydney and had been there for the last 2 months.

I was playing pool in the pub and got talking to a guy from Manchester. He told me he was sharing digs with a guy called Loz who was looking for his friend, Johnny Mac. *That's me*, I said, so we went back to his digs to surprise Loz and we celebrated well into the night. What a stroke of luck!

Loz and I decided to get digs together and a few weeks later we moved into a very nice place run by a middle-aged Dutch woman who served minced beef for breakfast. There were four other English blokes in this boarding house and we made friends with them almost straight away. It's funny; we talk about integration but all you want to do when you move to a foreign country is hang around with people from your own country and culture. It gives you a sense of familiarity and security until you settle in to your new surroundings.

The four guys we met were long-time friends from Stoke Newington, London. Paul was 19, blonde, good-looking and really friendly. Eric was 20, small with a dry sense of humour. Peter, his younger brother, 19, acted and looked older than Eric, and Terry, 19, the intelligent member of their group. We would all socialise together and eventually we all worked for the same firm, Ever Ready Hire Company.

This firm erected and hired lift towers for the outside of tall buildings in the centre of Sydney. We were riggers, and had to erect these structures, which would sometimes reach three or four hundred feet. This was hard and dangerous work. At first I was scared of heights, but after a few months I became as reckless as the others. Sometimes when we had reached the top of a tower, say about 250ft and it came to lunchtime we would race down the tower and the last person down had to pay for the beers. It was hard work but we were well paid, we were young and we used to party like mad at the weekends. This was the beginning of a great adventure.

It was a great time in our young lives. Loz, the four London lads and I moved to Bondi Beach, one of the most famous beaches in the world. We moved to a flat less than 500 yards from the beach – well, we called it a flat but it was more of a bedsit with a kitchen area curtained off; the bathroom was down the hallway and shared with the rest of the block. We were to live in 19 Lamrock Avenue for the next twelve months. Six of us in one room, so there wasn't much privacy if you wanted to bring a girl back for a romantic evening – no chance of that.

It was an idyllic life for a young man in 1970. We would get up at around 6am, go for a swim on Bondi Beach, go to work until 3pm then back to the beach, then the pub, come home, have a few joints then the same the next day. Weekends were party time, having fun – it's what young people do.

After about six months of living in Bondi we met a white Jamaican guy with red hair and fair skin, but when he talked he sounded like a Rastafarian. He was born and raised in Kingston, Jamaica from a white working class family. He had smuggled some very strong grass into Australia and was about to share it with us, but little did we know the stuff he had was about ten times stronger than anything we had ever taken before.

It was a sunny Sunday afternoon, we had all been to the pub and came back to the flat to relax and share a few joints. It wasn't unpleasant in the beginning. I got the giggles, then the munchies, so we went out and bought lots of ice cream - we were having a fabulous day. Later in the evening we decided to get an early night, as we had to work the next day. It was about midnight when I got to bed but I couldn't sleep, still a bit high I thought. Then I started to hallucinate - Paul who was sleeping next to me was now standing in front of me with a brightly coloured aura around him. I told him to stop messing around and go to sleep but when I looked again he was lying next to me snoring away. I was seeing things and I didn't like it. Inside I started to panic. I was afraid something was happening to me, that I was going mad. I woke Paul up and told him I was afraid and that I felt panicky, he just told me not to be daft and went back to sleep. I lay there getting more and more paranoid. I got up and dressed and went for a walk, hoping that this feeling would soon go with some fresh air. It must have been about 2am, although I had lost track of time. Walking along Campbell Parade, the promenade in Bondi, I was convinced it was Southport UK; this made me feel more like I was losing my mind. I had to get to a hospital and the nearest one was Bondi Junction, which was about two miles away.

Because of my paranoia I decided to hide any form of identification that would help the police identify me and charge me with drug offences. I stuffed my driver's licence and membership cards under a phone box. I then got a taxi to the hospital. At reception they asked what was wrong with me, I told them I thought I was going mad. The receptionist then asked my name and address. I couldn't even remember these simple details. *I am going mad!* I started to panic so she called for a doctor to attend me straight away. The nurse took me into a cubicle and two minutes later a young doctor arrived. He told me to calm down and asked me why I thought I was going mad. I told him I had been smoking marijuana and it was driving me insane. He then gave me a shot of Valium and immediately I felt so much better and more or less back to normal. I was not going mad after all. This was long before research into the effects of cannabis so they had no idea why it was causing me anxiety. The doctor referred me to a psychiatrist, who just told me that if I stopped smoking any drugs I should be fine. I didn't take his advice and the consequences were to come.

After living in Bondi for about a year, Loz and I decided we should see a bit more of Australia, after all it is a huge country. So we left our jobs, telling the rest of the lads to keep the flat going as we would be back in a few months. We headed to the state of Victoria to an area called Mildura. We had no money for hotels or any decent accommodation, so we slept where we could and we hitchhiked. Sleeping rough in the Australian bush can be very scary and dangerous. I remember the first night we slept on the veranda of a school and a huge spider crawled over my sleeping bag. That was it, I was awake for the rest of the night, whereas Loz was sleeping like a baby. Also the noises coming out of the bush! It was worse than living in the middle of a city; you could hear all sorts of animal sounds: crickets, dingo's, parakeets, owls... it was like an open zoo. It took us three days to get to our destination, a fruit-picking farm. It was full of drifters, students, guys on the run from the law and Pommies out for a bit of Australian bush experience. We were housed in breezeblock cubicles with no doors and bunk beds. Lying awake on the first night in there was like being in a bush tucker trial (something we have on TV now in a programme called *I'm a Celebrity Get Me Out of Here*)

As we lay on our bunks watching the spiders and lizards crawl all over the room, we heard some drunken guys coming back from the pub. It was about 2am. They were giggling and whispering, and the next thing we knew, a 6 foot snake was thrown into our bunk, landing on me. I, of course, screamed like a true Pom and threw the snake off me and onto Loz, who was braver than me and managed to get it out of harm's way. The guys outside were in stitches. The next day we described the snake to one of the farm hands and he said it sounded like a tiger snake, quite deadly. If bitten, we could have been very ill or even dead. Well that was enough for us to get some wood and make a door for our hut to keep the wildlife out. That didn't stop the drunken revellers from having their fun though. They started to put spiders and other small deadly creatures under the door. These blokes were maniacs – they had been working on this farm for too long and so had we. Within a month we were on our way back to Sydney and the safety of the city.

We had to hitch hike back to Sydney, so Loz and I stood at the roadside with our thumbs out waiting for a dream lift all the way back to Sydney. No such luck. After four hours in the heat some farmer who was going just 50 miles up the road picked us up. He dropped us off in the middle of nowhere. It was about 38° centigrade in the shade, and there was none. The area off the road was very desert-like, hardly any trees or vegetation. After about three hours, we saw a huge truck in the distance heading towards us. There was this heat haze at the end of the road and clouds of dust coming off the truck. This truck heading towards us is what they call a wagon train. It was a huge Mack unit pulling about four twenty-foot trailers. For these things to come to a stop they need to break about half a mile before.

Well this monster was not stopping, but as the truck passed us honking its mega-loud horn and covering us with red dust, we noticed something shiny being thrown out of the window. When the dust had settled we ran to see what had been ejected from the truck. When we reached it we couldn't believe what it was. It was like some Aussie beer commercial. It was a six-pack of ice-cold Foster's lager. What a result – just what we needed. The lager lasted about 5 minutes and no vehicles had passed us since the truck. Another two hours went by and in the distance we saw dust, which meant another car or truck was coming. We noticed it was a car from a mile away and it was being driven somewhat erratically. In fact it was zig-zagging from side to side and nearly hit us as it passed us. About 500 yards up the road, we noticed its break lights came on and it started reversing back to us in the same zigzag fashion.

It came to a stop and the rear passenger doors opened and a voice said, "Get in the fuckin' car, boys."

So we did. We were saved – or so we thought. The driver and his mate were two drunken true blue Aussies. They had cans of lager in their hands and were eating rabbit or some other creature from the bush. They didn't even ask us where we were heading; in fact we couldn't get a word in edgeways. But they were generous; they gave us some beer and some of this animal they were eating.

Twenty minutes into the journey they still hadn't really spoken to us when one of the Aussies said, "Anyway, where the fuck are you goin?"
Loz replied, "Sydney, but anywhere on the way will do."

All of a sudden the driver braked so hard we were nearly in the front seat with them. The two Aussies looked at one another with horror on their faces.

The driver screamed, "George, we've picked up a couple of Poms."

It was as if we had the black plague. They grabbed the beer and food off us, pushed open the door and said, "Get the fuck out, you Pommie bastards."

And we did, back on the road, only now it was pitch black. We had a sleepless night listening to the dingos and other creatures in the bush. Luckily the next morning we got a ride from a vicar and his wife all the way to Sydney. We slept all the way back.

The Tasman Sea

Back from the bush, Loz and I decided to get a flat together. We chose to stay in Bondi because that's where all the young people hung out – and the prettiest girls. Talking of pretty girls, the block of flats we moved into is where I met my first wife, Jasia. She and her friend would walk past our door every morning and say hi. Jasia was a very attractive and stylish 17 year old, intelligent and strong in her views and opinions for her age – my type of girl. I asked her out and we hit it off in many ways: music, clothes, sense of humour and very attracted to each other. We spent more and more time together but I still had no thoughts of settling down and having a family, after all, I was only 20.

Loz and the London lads said they were thinking of moving to Coogee and getting a house together and did I want to come? They must have thought that I wanted to move in with Jasia. Although I felt very strongly for Jasia I didn't want to give up my freedom just yet. So I said I would be joining my mates in Coogee.

Coogee was only about five miles from Bondi so it was easy to carry on my relationship with Jasia. The house in Coogee was great for the five of us: Loz, Peter, Paul, Eric, Terry, and me. We had parties nearly every Saturday night, in fact we were quite well known for them. I had my very memorable 21st there which went on for a couple of days I think. Because we all worked for the same company we would get up for work at about 6am on a beautiful summer's day and stick on Creedence Clearwater Revival's *Willy and the Poor Boys* at full blast and dance around the house eating our breakfast. The poor next door neighbours.

We'd been living in the house in Coogee for about six months and we had a party one Sunday night for a friend of ours who was returning to the UK. His name was Bill and he was a Scot. He said he was going back home because people like him, red hair and freckles, shouldn't live in a country that burned your skin to a crisp and gave you blisters. This was before skin cancer scares, so he was right to go home. The morning after the party, myself, Peter, Loz, Eric and another guy called Tony decided to take the day off work and take Bill to his ship that was due to sail at about noon. It was 6am, a hot sunny day, the sort Bill didn't like. We drove down to Circular Quay where his ship *The Oronsay* was sailing. The bars by the docks were open for shift workers and so on, so we thought we'd carry on the leaving celebrations.

We walked in the bar and it was packed, like a Saturday night, not a Monday morning. This early drinking was leading us into some trouble; we started drinking at about 8am and by the time Bill had to board ship we were a little merry. Bill said we could get passes to come on board to say our final farewell, so we did and headed straight to the bar. The bar was packed with passengers heading home to the UK, it was like a party. At about 11am the tannoy fed out a message: *Will all visitors to the Oronsay please disembark, as we are preparing to set sail. Thank you.*

Bill said, "Right lads, thanks for coming down to see me off."
Loz: "That's fine, we'll stay a little longer, get off at the last minute."

After 15 minutes the tannoy kicked in again: "This is the final request for visitors to the ship to disembark, as we are preparing to leave Sydney."

Peter said, "Right, lads let's go."
I said, "Why don't we go to New Zealand for the week?"

Loz, Eric, and a guy called Tony thought it was a good idea.

Paul said, "You're mad. What about work? The house? Girlfriends?"

I had just found out that Jasia was pregnant but we were so drunk we never thought of the consequences. So Paul, Terry and Peter left mumbling about how stupid we were and that we were crazy. The rest of us thought it was a hoot as we sailed under the Sydney Harbour Bridge – a bright sunny day and we were at sea!

It got to about 9 o'clock and most of the passengers had gone to their cabins or to meals. We were still in the bar with Bill and a few girls we had latched onto. Bill thought we had lost the plot, but said he would hide one of us in his cabin. So Tony went with him, as he was a good friend of his. Eric just wondered off somewhere. He was always a bit like that, Eric; he had been smoking dope all day and was away with the fairies. Loz got the offer of a place with one of the girls we had met. So I just sat in the bar with the rest of the people. One by one they went off to bed. No offer for me to be hidden in a cabins - they didn't want to get in any trouble - so I just sat there on my own drinking.

It got to about 3am. The bar was closed and I had fallen asleep on one of the long seats. I was woken by this guy in uniform, one of the duty officers. I was feeling a bit sick, but didn't know whether to put it down to the drink or the ship's movement. I do suffer badly from seasickness. The officer was trying to move me on, a bit like a policeman with a down and out on a park bench.

"Can I take you to your cabin, sir? You can't sleep here."

I was feeling so ill I didn't care where he took me as long as I could lie down.

"Yes thank you," I said.
"And what number is your cabin, sir?" I made up a number.
"And what deck would that be on?"
"Er, can't remember," I slurred.

So we stumbled about the ship looking for my fictitious cabin. After about 40 minutes of waking people up and me throwing up every five minutes I had to own up; I just wanted to lie down.

"Listen Officer," I said, "I shouldn't be on this ship. I came to see a friend off and I have stayed on board."

Then the officer's attitude changed.

"Right," he said, grabbed me by the arm and frog-marched me to the Captain's quarters. He had to wake up the Captain, who was not very happy. I couldn't care less. I was feeling so bad if they had shot me it would have been a blessing. After a short discussion between the Captain and the Officer the only word I heard was *brig* and that's where the officer took me. He unlocked the door and shoved me in. *Great* – there were four bunks in there and I dived onto the first one. I heard the door being opened and a bucket was slung in – which I badly needed.

I awoke at about 8am. The door was unlocked and Eric was standing there with a big grin on his face.

"So they got you as well, Macca."

I sat up still feeling like my head was about to explode and my stomach was completely empty.

"How did they find you?" I said to Eric.
"I must have wandered into the nursery and there was a Wendy House so I fell asleep in there. A little kid woke me up this morning then went off to tell the teacher that a big giant was asleep in the Wendy House. Of course she didn't believe him but then six of the other kids came in and started screaming and that's when she went for help."

We looked around the brig. It was about 10x10 with four bunks and the bucket. It had a small barred porthole that looked out onto the first class deck tennis courts, a really unusual place for a ship's lock up.

The journey from Sydney to Auckland takes three days across the Tasman, and it can be very rough. On the second day, Loz was caught. The girl he was staying with threw him out of her cabin, so he had nowhere to hide. Tony was still free to roam the decks. On that second day in the brig, one of the officers said he was taking us below decks to feed us. As we were now classed as stowaways they had to keep us locked up until they reached Auckland, then we were to be handed over to the authorities and dealt with through the New Zealand courts. The officer handcuffed us together and led us below decks to eat with the crew. We sat amongst the crew to eat our breakfast and we were the centre of attention, the crew asking us where we were from, why we stowed away and so on.

The officer would not release our handcuffs to eat so we had to time the spooning in of our food or we were pulling each other's forks out of our mouths. The crew thought this was hilarious. As we were being led back to the brig, some of the crew members offered to hide us in their cabins if we managed to escape, but unfortunately that never happened. That night we were sitting talking about what would happen when we reached New Zealand. We had jobs, a house and I had a girlfriend who was pregnant and there was no way I could get word to her that I hadn't deserted her intentionally.

At about 9pm the brig door opened and Tony stepped in.

The officer said, "Is that it now or are there more of you?"

"No," I said, "You've got the set."

This was our last night in the brig together because at noon tomorrow we would be docking in Auckland. At about midnight we heard someone calling us from outside the porthole. It was some of the crew. They had brought us some supplies to celebrate our last night on board. They passed cigarettes, whisky, food and some grass through the porthole. Well what a party we had. I think we passed out at about 6am. When I woke up at about 9 o'clock Eric was at the porthole with his arm out of the window shouting to the first class passengers playing deck tennis. They must have wondered what the hell was going on, this long-haired bearded bloke shouting, *Help me, I've been kidnapped!* Two minutes later the brig door opened and the Second Officer came in to see what was going on. He couldn't believe his eyes: four prisoners looking hungover with empty whisky bottles and food leftovers strewn across the floor of the brig.

Porridge

We docked in Auckland Harbour at noon. We waited for the police to come on board to escort us to the police station, to be charged with stowing away and intending to enter a country illegally. None of which were true – it was a stupid prank that went badly wrong. The police put us in a Black Maria so all we saw of Auckland was through the barred windows of the van. When we reached the station they charged us, finger printed us, and took mug shots. Because it was a Friday we had to stay in the police lock up until Monday morning for our moment in court.

Monday morning came and we were taken in the van to the High Court in Auckland. Our case came up second, and the judge we found out later was the meanest one you could get on the circuit. We pleaded guilty to being on board *The Oronsay* with no tickets or passports, but pleaded not guilty to trying to enter New Zealand illegally. The judge asked us for any mitigating circumstances. We told him that it was a stupid prank, that we had jobs and commitments back in Sydney, that we would pay back the fare to P&O Lines and we were very sorry for what we had done. The judge found us guilty for the stowing away charge but not guilty on the illegal entry charge. We thought great, a fine and a slap on the wrist; we could fly back tomorrow and all would be well. The judge then summed up our sentence.

'You are sentenced to three months' detention and then deportation by available means."

We were in shock.

"What is deportation by available means?" Loz asked.

"It means," said the judge, "you will serve your sentence of three months, then after that we will ask the P&O Line if they will transport you back to Sydney."

"What if they don't?" I asked.

"We will ask the company every time one of their ships visit Auckland if they will take you back and if after one year none of them will oblige, we will repatriate you."

"So we could end up doing a year for just stowing away?" Eric said.

"Yes, I am afraid so," said the judge.

Eric then shouted out, "I hope you rot in hell, you horrible old bastard!"

"Take them down" said the judge.

So that's where we went, down the stairs of the courtroom into a holding cell, then into the prison van. We shared the van with other convicted prisoners of the day, a drug dealer, an arsonist and a big Maori guy convicted of GBH. We spoke very little on our way to Mount Eden Maximum Security Prison, our new home for the next three months.

It was about 6 pm when we arrived so we had missed our dinner. Altogether there were about nine new inmates to be processed. After handing over all our personal possessions and clothes we had a short interview with a doctor and a social worker to assess our health and mental state. Just before we were allocated our cells, the Senior Warden gave us a lecture on the rules and how to survive your prison sentence. When he had finished he asked if we had any questions.

I very stupidly said, "I suffer with claustrophobia and I don't like confined spaces."

The warden and the rest of the prisoners, including my friends, just fell about laughing.

After the laughter had died down, the warden said, "Well, we will soon cure you of that."

The prison was Victorian and based on British prison architecture. In fact, most of the Prison Officers were from the UK. We were then led to our cells. I was hoping to share with one of my mates, but no chance – we were separated. I was placed in a cell with a complete stranger, the cell was about 12ft by 6ft with no toilet or sink. It had a small window high up, barred with frosted glass. The cell smelled of this man's sweat and body odour. He was about 35, which was old to me at that time, white and of stocky build. Not a very friendly chap, he just grunted something about the top bunk being his and the piss pot was in the corner if I needed it during the night. After about ten minutes I started to cry, my claustrophobia kicking in and fear filling my head. I started to bang on the cell door and shout for a warden but nobody came. After about ten minutes my cellmate told me to: *Shut the fuck up or he would kill me.* This made me worse. I started screaming for the Warden to come and help me as I was about to be murdered. This got the Warden's attention; he unlocked the door and asked me what the problem was. I told him I was scared of the guy in the cell and was suicidal. He said there was nothing he could do until morning and he would book me in with the Welfare Officer. I calmed down a little and dropped onto my bunk, hoping this nightmare would go away.

After a sleepless night we were woken at 6am for what they call 'slopping out', which meant emptying your piss pot. You would form a long queue along a metal gangway, and because we were on the first floor there was a net in between the gangways to prevent prisoners from throwing themselves off or throwing objects to the floor below. All human life was in this queue; fat, thin, black, white, ugly, handsome – but mostly ugly. I spotted Loz across the gangway: he waved and I waved back. This caused some of the prisoners to heckle and cheer. Because we had not been to the prison barber's yet our hair was still long, shoulder length; after all it was the seventies.

Back to the cell, and at 8am we went out onto the landing for breakfast. You would queue up again for breakfast and then eat it in your cell. The only time you left your cell was for slopping out, breakfast, lunch, one

John McArdle

hour in the prison yard for exercise, evening meal, then lights out at 8pm. So I spent about 23 hours locked up with a not-so-perfect stranger, who I had absolutely nothing in common with, who was not very talkative and slightly aggressive.

Because this was our first day, we had to continue with our introduction to prison life. The four of us were escorted to the barber's together, and we swapped stories about our first night. Loz was sharing with some guy that was doing ten years for armed robbery, Eric was sharing with a fraudster, and Tony was with a lunatic that wouldn't stop talking all night. He should have been in the psychiatric block. The barber, well butcher really, gave us a number 2 haircut, no skill involved, just set the clipper and shaved away. Eric was made a fool of: they cut just half of his hair off and let him walk around for a bit to amuse the other prisoners. Eric didn't seem to mind – if he was making someone laugh he was happy. And I was happy too at the end of the day. I had been to see the Welfare Officer and told him how unhappy I was with my unsociable cellmate, and he arranged for me to share a cell with Eric – hurray! The first week went by very slowly. There didn't seem to be any rehabilitation going on here; it was just a 'bang em up' mentality.

We got to know some of the more approachable prisoners during our hour's exercise each day. They would all give you the same advice: keep your gob shut and do your time – and our time compared to some of them was a spit in the ocean. The Vietnam War was in full swing at the time so you had young guys in there who had broken the law protesting about that conflict. One guy was doing seven years for blowing up Royal New Zealand Air force planes in their hangars at the airbase. They caught him because he had sent a note to the national papers saying it was a protest against New Zealand's involvement in the Vietnam War. The police traced the letter back to him – not a very clever student. We thought *we* were in jail for a trivial crime but one guy we talked to got 28 days for saying *Bullshit* in public; he was also a student protesting against the war.

After about a month we knew who to talk to and who to avoid. The main ones to avoid were the sexual predators. These are not gay men or sexual deviants; outside of prison these were normal, heterosexual men but on the inside they would use anyone for sex – especially young good-looking men. I managed to avoid being used or raped but poor Eric came very close to being a 'bitch' as they say inside. A huge six foot five tattooed, shaven-headed male nurse took a fancy to Eric. Being angelic of face, Eric seemed to attract this sort of person. Let's call this bloke Neanderthal Barry. Well Barry tried everything to get his hands on Eric; he said if Eric was to go sick and get moved to the medical section of the prison he would look after him (of course he would). Eric was much brighter than we gave him credit for. He told Barry if he could wait for 4 months he would be all his, Eric was thinking that we would be out by then if all went well and as Barry didn't know our sentence he agreed to this.

One day we were called to the Senior Warden's office. We were hoping it was an early release, but no such luck. He told us we were to be moved to the kitchen cells so we could spend the rest of our two months working in the kitchen. This was a privileged job because you weren't stuck in your cell for 23 hours a day but were in the kitchens preparing and serving the food. Plus, the cells by the kitchens were so much better – they had toilets and a sink. Although we had only been inside for a month it seemed like a year, but now we had something to do, our time would go faster. The other guys in the kitchen were a lot older and in for more serious crimes, but they were ok with us. After we had served the prisoners their meals we would then all sit around a table together and have our meal.

Usually no one ever asked what you were in for but this day, one of the guys asked us what we had done to end up in here. We looked at each other, then Tony not wanting to sound like a wimp, said; "Armed robbery."
"What did you rob'?" asked the prisoner.
"We held up the finance office on a ship," said Tony.
"Bit stupid that isn't it? Nowhere to run!" said the prisoner

Then the chef, who knew what we were really in for, said, "They never robbed anything, they just stowed away and got caught."

Laughter all round. It was good in a way because after that we were treated like a joke, no threat to anyone. The Scouse Family Robinson they called us, because two of us were from Liverpool.

Each day we would help prepare the meals, peel potatoes, shell peas, that sort of thing, then we would take some tables out onto the landings and serve the food from there. The other prisoners would come out of their cells at meal times then take the food back to their cells to eat. Sometimes if a particular prisoner was troublesome or violent, they would have to wait until the rest of the prisoners had been served and gone back to their cells and then were let out individually, as they could not mix with other inmates.

One particular day, after we had served the majority of inmates, the wardens told us the next prisoner we would be serving breakfast to was a very nasty piece of work and would ask for more - but under no circumstances were we to give him more than was allocated. I was on bacon, Eric was on eggs, Tony was on beans and Loz was on toast. After the main prisoners were banged up, one of the screws unlocked the cell to let this unsavoury character out. He was short and stocky with a boxer's nose, tattoos of swallows on his neck and he looked pissed off. There were about six wardens and us four serving the breakfast. Things started off well: I served him his bacon, no problem and so on until it came to Loz on the toast. Loz placed the allocated slice of toast on this guy's plate.

He asked Loz for another slice.

Loz said, "Sorry, you're only allowed one."

"I don't give a fuck what I am allowed," he replied. "Stick another one on there.'"

So Loz obliged and gave this maniac another slice of toast.

Then one of the screws stepped in and said to Loz, "Take it back – he's only allowed the one."

"Touch that toast and I'll chop your fuckin' hand off," said Mr Nasty.

Loz was shitting himself and I was thinking, *I'm glad it's not me.*

Loz said, "Sorry, mate, if it was up to me you could have ten pieces of toast."

This guy's eyes were looking right through Loz; he was one scary bloke. The screw could see that there was no way Loz was going to take that toast back, so he went to take it. The prisoner grabbed his hand, twisted it, then butted him square on the nose. The rest of the screws dived in to restrain the madman and bundled him back to his cell with a good beating. The landing was strewn with food and mess, which we had to clean up. We then heard the rest of the prisoners banging their metal cups against the cell doors and shouting, *Screw brutality!*

Life in Mount Eden prison was never dull. There was always something happening; you would hear of a stabbing or an attempted escape or a suicide – it was a dramatic place to be. But nothing prepared us for what happened one Saturday morning during our exercise break.

The exercise yard was about the size of a football field with areas for playing football or weight-lifting, the sort of prison yard you see in American films. This yard had a huge 40ft wall at one end and on the other side of that wall was a highway – you could hear the traffic. We were sitting about 300 yards from the big wall, talking and listening to some inmate telling us that he was the best robber in Auckland and what jobs he was going to do when he got out. So much for rehabilitation. Suddenly a huge cheer went up over by the wall and most of the prisoners in the yard were heading over there, so we decided to go too. When we reached the wall there was pandemonium, inmates grabbing whatever was being thrown over the wall. We soon found out what it was: cartons of cigarettes, bottles of whisky, cans of beer, chocolate, nudie magazines, sweets and even some ganja. Prisoners were grabbing everything they could. We were stuffing cigs up our jumpers, eating the chocolate, and drinking the alcohol as fast as we could, because we knew the contraband would be confiscated. It took

John McArdle

30 seconds for the screws to realise what was going on, and they got us into a line to search us. Along that line, people were stuffing themselves silly because it would soon be taken away. We did manage to smuggle some cigs in but most of the stuff was taken off us.

Deportation

Eric and I were sitting in our cell one morning, just a week short of our three month sentence. Suddenly the door was unlocked and one of the wardens popped his head in.

"Get your shit together – you're going back to Sydney in the morning."

It was true, a P&O Line ship had agreed to transport us back to Sydney. Hooray! I've never been strongly religious, especially after I thought God had taken you from us so early. But a few weeks prior to news of our early release I had prayed to God to get us out of this place and it looked like he had answered me. The next morning, we got our clothes and belongings back, plus 10 NZ dollars, wages for working in the kitchen. We said our goodbyes to the inmates we befriended. They were sad and jealous to see us go – after all most of them were in for a very long time.

On the ship we were given DBS quarters. This is usually reserved for distressed British seamen, sailors who had either missed their ships or jumped ship and had to be repatriated. The crew invited us to the 'Pig', which is their name for the ship's bar. Well that's all that I remember of the three-day trip back to Sydney. After three months of abstaining from alcohol and with the rolling of the ship, I was so ill I stayed in my bunk for the whole trip. It did not affect my three friends; they were out every night getting plastered. They would come back about 2am eating bacon butties and smoking. They thought it was hilarious: they would offer me drink and food and I would let out some grunting or retching sound and they would double up laughing.

When we landed in Sydney, I had lost about one and a half stone and was still feeling ill. What now? Where did we go? All we had were the clothes we stood up in and ten New Zealand dollars each. There was only one place we could go: back to the house we rented before we set of on our lost weekend. The Sydney taxi driver was really pissed off when we paid him in NZ dollars, but what could he do?

We walked down the path to the house that held all our worldly goods and knocked on the door. A strange man answered.

We moved to enter the house and this man says, "Where do you think you're going?"

"Inside," said Loz. "We live here."

"No you don't," replied the man. "I've been living here with my wife and kids for the past two months. You must be the guys who lived here before and ended up in a Kiwi nick."

"That's us," I said. "So where is Peter and Paul?"

"Back to Bondi," says the guy. "I've got their address somewhere."

The bloke came back with an address for Peter and Paul, who now lived in Bondi Junction. So we stood outside our old house with no possessions, my car nowhere in sight, $20 between us and homeless. Also we had to get a taxi with the Kiwi money the Aussies think is worthless.

We arrived at Peter and Paul's tiny bedsit in Bondi junction and they were really pleased to see us. So they went to the bottle shop (or off licence as we call it) and bought lots of grog – the Aussie word for beer – and celebrated our homecoming. The story after we left on our lost weekend came out. Paul had thought we would get a rap on the knuckles and get sent back to Sydney. After a couple of weeks, he knew that was not going to happen. Peter and Paul had to get another place to live, as they couldn't afford to stay in the house. Whilst moving stuff from the house to their new flat someone had burgled the house stealing most of our possessions.

So we were now a blank sheet, no job, no money, no home and no possessions. An old friend, thinking I would be rotting in some foreign gaol, had taken my car.

My next important mission was to find Jasia, my pregnant girlfriend. She was staying at some friends of ours, a really great couple, Alex and Cordulla. I turned up at midnight and she opened the door. She let me in. She thought I had run away on purpose to get away from my responsibilities as a future father. I felt so sorry for her: she was so young and afraid of telling her parents that she was pregnant. I told her I would stand by her. I moved in with her and things slowly got back to normal. I got a job and a car and life started going well again for a time.

But then I started to feel anxious about becoming a father at 21. Jasia was scared too, not just about the birth but about telling her parents. I didn't know if I could face up to my responsibilities and we discussed separating and having the baby adopted. We decided that was the best thing to do. Loz, Ray and his girlfriend were going to Tasmania fruit picking and asked if I wanted to join them. I accepted their offer. It was a tearful goodbye with Jasia. Not only was I leaving her but I was abandoning my unborn child.

We travelled in my Mini Moke to Melbourne and were going to get a ferry from there to Tasmania. All the way on the journey to Melbourne I couldn't stop feeling guilty about leaving Jasia and the baby. I couldn't get it off my mind. When we got to Melbourne I phoned Jasia, but she had gone into labour. That was it – I couldn't stand it anymore. I told my friends I was going back to Sydney to be with Jasia. They wished me luck and off I went.

The distance from Melbourne to Sydney is approximately 600 miles and it took me 14 hours. I arrived in Sydney and went straight to the hospital, into the ward where Jasia was. Jasia was in bed, holding this tiny little baby with bright orange hair. It was a boy. We called him Justin. I never regret going back to be with Jasia. I couldn't stand the thought of my child being given away to a stranger. He's turned into a lovely young man but more about him later on.

One night I was round the lads' flat having a drink, watching television when the 'Call Up' ad came on. At this time in Australia, 1970, they were committed along with the USA and New Zealand to the Vietnam War. So 19 to 25 year-olds were eligible for conscription. This included all male British citizens residing in Australia. Once a month the government would use this lottery type method of picking men to be conscripted. They would place balls in a rotating glass dome and they would be released one at a time. The first ball was the day of birth, second was month and third was year.

As we all sat there, waiting to see which poor bastards were going to Vietnam, my numbers came up. The presenter picked the balls out: 16, then 8, then 49. He ended with the words: *All men with this birth date must register within the next month for call up for the Australian Armed Services.* There was a stunned silence in the room. They knew that was my birth date – they were all at my 21st.

Eric was first to speak. "Looks like you're fucked, John."
"I can't believe it," I said. "I don't want to fight in some war that I don't even support or die so young in a foreign land."
We spent the rest of the evening discussing a way out of this horrible situation. Being a conscientious objector was ruled out because that meant going to jail, and I couldn't bear the thought of that. I have would sooner died.
Eric said, "Why don't you cut off a toe or finger?", "You're joking, aren't you?" I replied.
Finally Loz came up with a solution. He knew a guy who was taking on riggers and scaffolders in Papua New Guinea. I could get out of Oz for a while and let things quieten down a little – they may even forget about me. That was it. That's what I would do. I would go to NG for six months, make some money, come back and Jasia and I would get married.

You Never Said Goodbye

I put this to Jasia that night and she agreed to it. The sacrifice of me working away was worth it for our future. I got the job and left for NG. We flew out of Sydney on a small passenger plane seating about 20 workers bound for Bougainville, part of the Solomon Islands. Flying time was only 2 hours but the mostly Aussie workers on board got stuck into the beer, and after an hour they had drunk the plane dry. When they were told there was no more beer they started to stamp their feet causing the small plane to rock about. After ignoring requests from the pilot to stop, the air hostess brought a shot of whisky for everyone. I didn't drink mine as I was a little air sick. After about ten minutes everyone but me and the aircrew were fast asleep. They had laced the whisky with sleeping pills to control the unruly passengers – and it worked. We landed on the grass airstrip, the plane came to a standstill, engines off…and all you could hear was snoring.

This place I had come to work in was a tropical island paradise. It had everything you could dream of: swaying palm trees, golden beaches, clear blue sea with tropical fish. We were billeted in air-conditioned rooms just a stone's throw away from the beach and this would be my home for the next three months. The reason all these foreign workers were here was to build a power station on the coast to supply the copper mine in the mountains. This beautiful island was rich in minerals such as gold and copper and was being exploited by the Australian government. In fact this whole island had been exploited by a number of colonialists since French explorer Captain Louis Bougainville discovered it in 1768. Then a succession of invaders looted the island, the Germans, British and Dutch all playing their part. During World War Two the Japanese army occupied the island from 1942 to 1944. They left the place in a mess and many islanders were killed in the conflict. Since that time it has been under Australian administration.

The workers consisted of welders, pipe fitters, electricians, riggers/scaffolders and carpenters from every corner of the globe. It was a real multinational work force. On my first day of work we travelled through the jungle by truck. The dirt road to the power station was an interesting journey. It was 7am, the sun was already high, and the bush was full of wildlife, beautiful flowers and plants. We would pass through villages with grass-roofed huts, and the children of the village would run alongside the truck waving and asking in pidgin English for fresh oranges or sweets. It was a delightful journey to work and how different from the city commute.

The indigenous people of this beautiful island were so friendly and welcoming to us, despite having every right to be hostile for what was happening to their culture and land. They were always laughing and smiling, and men would openly hold hands with other men. They saw no wrong in this, it was simply showing their affection to friends. Of course we westerners thought they were weird, when in fact we were the ignorant ones. The women of the village went about their everyday business topless, except on Sundays, when they would wear a bra for church. Christian missionaries had been on the island since 1902. There was one very strict rule on the Island; the local women were out of bounds. The site manager warned us that as long as we respected their laws and customs we would be welcome. One particular German worker disrespected their law and had an affair with a native girl. His head was found on a spiked stick on the beach. That was enough for me. I was afraid to speak to a local girl for more than a minute.

Life was great on Bougainville. Even though we worked hard, the sun shone all the time and we swam in the turquoise blue Indian Ocean every day. You would probably have to pay a lot of money to experience that today. One of the guys from Sydney had brought some marijuana to the island to keep us all happy, so we decided to plant some of the seeds in the bush to see if we could keep up a supply. It worked: the plants spread and we had a never-ending supply. There were no police on the island so we had no worries about breaking the law, if there was a law that is. At the weekend we would set up some huge speakers on the beach and listen to Led Zeppelin at full volume and smoke lots of ganja. It was paradise.

One Saturday night I was sitting in the outside bar with a few friends. This bar in fact had no indoors – it was all outside. It consisted of about 60 picnic style tables with a sand floor, surrounded by dense jungle. It was a very humid starry night. There were about 100 men in this jungle beer garden. The floor was a carpet of empty stubby beer bottles; no one returned them to the bar, and they just used to throw their empties on the ground. There was a mixture of Europeans and black workers from Port Moresby. It was very noisy, as you can imagine, as the more people drank the louder they got. All of a sudden some of the chattering stopped; the guys on our table were still in conversation. Why had it gone quiet? One of the Port Moresby guys looked at me and then moved his eyes across to the edge of the jungle. It was now deadly silent.

We couldn't believe it. Had we been smoking too much weed? Tribesmen from the hills surrounded us. They had paint on their bodies and held spears, bows and arrows and blowpipes. It was really scary. Nobody moved. They just stood there, staring at us. One of the drunken Europeans shouted something to them but they didn't respond. In fact one of the Port Moresby guys gave him a filthy look as if to say *You're endangering our lives*. After a few minutes the tribesmen disappeared into the jungle as silently as they arrived. We found out later they were the Rotokas tribe from the mountains; they were curious and had come down to observe us. I don't know why. Maybe to size up the enemy or to see what strange people had invaded their island again. It was an experience I have never forgotten, both terrifying and wondrous at the same time.

I told you earlier that the local natives that worked alongside us were friendly and it is true that they would never harm you - but they would fight each other. Their fights were quite brutal; they would use rocks, sticks, bottles, and anything they could lay their hands on. It would not stop until one or the other was unconscious. It was just like in some British pubs on a Saturday night.

John McArdle

The power station we were building was a hive of activity from 8am to 6pm, with the noise of grinders, jackhammers, drills, and chain blocks pulling pipes into place. There were flashes from welding rods, sparks from the grinders and smoke from the cutting equipment. It was hard work but we were being paid well for it. The hours were long but there was nothing else to do. We didn't need to spend any money as the company, food, accommodation, medical care, and travel was paid for, so all your wages were just paid into your bank account. I was responsible for rigging up the scaffolding for the welders. I had two native trade assistants and we worked together really well. Sometimes these guys would go on walkabout for a couple of weeks without telling you. We were supposed to book them out so their very poor wages would be docked, but I and a couple of the other riggers would book them in and not inform the company. When the young trade assistants realised we were doing this they used to bring us gifts from their tribes. It would be some artefact that had been made in their villages.

One day we were working in the centre of the power station erecting some scaffolding when I noticed that the two trade assistants working with me had disappeared. *Not two on walkabout*, I thought. All of a sudden I began to feel dizzy. I had had nothing to drink the night before, so it wasn't a hangover. I then started to feel nauseous. *I must be coming down with some jungle lurgy.* One of my mates said he was feeling the same. We then looked to the outside of the power station and all the native workers were standing outside, waving and shouting for us to come out of the power station.

In their pidgin English they were shouting: "You die finish, him house power him fall down!" suddenly we understood what they were telling us and got out of there very fast. We had experienced an earth tremor, connected to the live volcano on the island Mount Bagona. Booking them in for their walkabouts had been worth it.

I shared a room with a friend of mine who had followed me out from Sydney. His name was Ray and he was from Nuneaton. The room we shared was about 10ft square, two single beds, a bedside table, and a small wardrobe each - so you can imagine how intimate it was. After work we would have an evening meal, maybe a quick pint and back to our room to read or write letters home. We would be asleep by say 10.30 at the latest as we had early starts every day except Sundays.

At 2.30am one morning, Ray's shouting and screaming awakened me. He thought he was going to die, and he was shivering like crazy. I took my blanket off and wrapped it around him, but it made no difference. I ran next door and asked one of the guys to stay with him whilst I ran for help. We had no phones and the medical centre was two miles away through the jungle and it was pitch black. I had no alternative; I had to get him some medical attention. I grabbed a torch and set off running through this frightening jungle. The fear I felt was so bad. All I could think of were snakes on the path waiting to bite me and poisonous spiders dropping down from the trees! I ran like the wind, singing and swearing to try and distract myself. The noises I could hear were from frogs, crickets, bats, and in my imagination, tigers. I must have run the fastest two miles ever. I reached the medical centre soaked in sweat, from fear and humidity, but mainly fear. The medical centre was like a small hospital with about 20 beds. There was a medic on night duty who was so laid back he was horizontal.

"Calm down," he said to me. "What's the problem?"

I told him what Ray's symptoms were and straight away he said, "Malaria."

We jumped in his ambulance and headed back to the camp. It was in fact malaria and Ray had to spend three weeks in hospital recovering.

I had been on the island for three months now and I was starting to miss Jasia and my friends back in Sydney. I had to finish my six-month contract to be entitled to all bonuses and benefits. If you left before this time you lost a lot of money and you had to pay for your own airfare back to the mainland.

A tragic accident happened on the island that was to affect me very badly. A crane was on its way to the power station, when it came off the road and ended upside down in a small stream. The cab with two young guys in it was submerged in the water. Some people from one of the villages went to their aid, but there was no way they could get them out and they drowned. I didn't know these men but it played on my mind. What a horrible way to die, trapped in a tiny cab with the water filling up and no way out. This incident really disturbed me. I couldn't get it out of my mind. I wasn't sleeping well and began to go in on myself. I became paranoid, *maybe I'm next*. I had it fixed in my mind that I was never going to get off this island and that I was going to die here like those two young guys. I came across as normal to my friends, but in my head I was going mad. It was like being in a dream with a kind of haze around me. I then started to hallucinate. I woke up in the middle of the night and saw a monkey on Ray's shoulder, and I screamed and woke him up. I told him there was a monkey on his shoulder. He said I had been smoking too much weed and he went back to sleep. I was losing it. I was on the edge of having a nervous breakdown. I had to get off this island. The next day I reported sick and told the medic what I was going through. He thought I was making it up to finish my contract early and claim the bonuses. After talking to my union rep and foreman, they eventually repatriated me back to Sydney.

I realised that smoking too much dope had given me psychosis and this breakdown was the result of it. I made myself a vow never to smoke marijuana ever again, and I can honestly say I never have.

I arrived back in Sydney safe and sound. My mind was still unclear; it was like living in this fog. I tried to explain to Jasia and she told me to see a doctor. I was referred to a psychiatrist but he wasn't much help so I hoped it would just go away on its own. Jasia, Justin and I were living in Alex and Cordulla's small flat which wasn't ideal so we had to make plans and quick. We decided to get married and move to Perth where we would start a new life. Jasia had told her parents, who were shocked at first but invited us to stay with them until I found a job and a place to rent. We were married at Sydney Registry office, attended by all our friends, including our son Justin. After a few days of saying goodbye to everyone, we boarded the Indian Pacific train bound for Perth 2,698 miles away. It was a fantastic journey. On our first night, we went back to our sleeper after dinner, looked out of the window onto a beautiful starlit night and watched the desert fly by.

We had a stop to make in Adelaide to visit Jasia's father, Hendrik. He had been separated from Jasia's mother since Jasia was 14. He was so pleased to see us, especially Justin, his first grandchild. Hendrik was Polish and shared a house with a Polish family. They were very hospitable to us, but a little bit wary of my appearance. I think because I had long hair and a beard, wore ripped denims, and flip-flops, they thought I was some drug-fuelled Hippy. They weren't far wrong. At the dinner table they were talking about me in Polish, so I asked Hendrik to translate. He told me they thought I looked like a degenerate. I told him to ask them if they thought that God was a degenerate too. *'Why do you ask that?'*

I replied, "Because you have a picture of him on the wall, with long hair and a beard and wearing sandals."

They all turned to look, and then turned back and we all just started laughing.

Hendrik was a very interesting guy. He had been imprisoned in Auschwitz during the Second World War and had experienced some pretty horrific things. It was sad to see this man who had gone through all that, to then lose his family again to divorce. But he was so proud and happy to have Justin his first grandson. We stayed with Hendrik for a few days and then we continued our journey onto Perth. I was looking forward to meeting the rest of Jasia's family.

I had written to my mother just after Justin was born to tell her she was a grandmother. Her reply came about three months later with a shock for me: she had given birth to her sixth child, Tricia, at the age of 43. She had met someone and they had got married. I had very mixed feelings about this, Dad; at first I thought she was being disloyal to you. But later I realised my mother's life had to go on and she was only young herself.

We arrived at Perth railway station and were met by Jasia's family. Her mum, Margaret ran to hug Jasia and Justin and then me. Angelo, her stepfather, a true Italian, shook my hand and said, "Welcome to the family.".

Her sisters Marisia, Michelle, and Brigit were fussing around Justin. We got to their home in Cobellup to stay with them until we could find a place of our own. They laid on a big supper for us and we were having a great celebration. Then something happened to me. I was feeling a little tired and I was still suffering from this weird head thing that had been going on since I left New Guinea. I lost consciousness for about 3 minutes, and then came around feeling sick and disorientated. Apparently I had had a seizure. They were all worried about me, so Margaret called an ambulance and they took me in for checks. They tested me for epilepsy but that was negative. The doctor put it down to stress and tiredness. I made my own conclusions and put it down to the drugs I had been using.

Staying with Angelo and Margaret was very nice and they were so hospitable, but we had to find our own place and I had to get a job. I got a job with a neon sign company, erecting signs all around Perth city centre. One day I received an official looking letter, with the Government logo on it. I opened it and it was from the Australian National Service Board. They had found me after one year on the run, so to speak. The letter stated that I had to report to the recruitment office in Perth within the next 7 days or I would be arrested for dodging the draft. *This is it*, I thought, *I could be in Vietnam in the next few months.*

Angelo said not to worry as I was married now with a child and I would be exempt. So I had some hope on the day I went to be assessed for the Australian Army. I arrived at the recruitment office feeling very scared indeed. After going through a medical, I then had an interview with an officer who asked if there was any reason that I would be unsuitable for being called up. I had a list as long as my face.

First of all I was against fighting in another country's war that I didn't believe in; secondly I had left one of Britain's elite regiments, the Paras, because I wasn't suited. Also I was married with a young child. And lastly I'd had an epileptic fit a few months back.

"Do you want me now?"

The officer replied, "I am sure we will find you something."

The bastard. He thinks I'm this hippy conscientious objector and he's going to have me.

On leaving, the sergeant on the desk said, "You should get your call up in about three weeks."

For the next three weeks I would come home from work, check the mail to see if that horrible government post mark was there. And then it came. Nearly all of Jasia's family were gathered round to see what the letter said. I opened it very slowly and read it out. They didn't want my services as a soldier in the Australian Army. *Yippee*! How we celebrated!!

Life was good. We had found a little house to rent in Fremantle, I had a decent job and the sun shone every day, even in the winter. Justin was 2 years old now but I was getting a little homesick – after all, I had been away from England for nearly four years. Jasia and I discussed going to the UK and we decided to save up and go for a couple of years. Jasia had family in Holland as that was where she was originally from so she would be able to see them. The job I was in paid all right, but not enough to save money. So I applied for a job on the Northwest Cape with a construction company. The money was good but it meant being away again for three months.

This job was very similar to the one I did in New Guinea; work all day, drink at the weekend and save money. The nearest town to the construction site was called Robourne, a real Aussie bush town, dirt streets, a pub/

hotel, and grocers. The pub was really rough. The felt on the pool table was ripped, half the balls were missing and most of the pool cues were broken in half and there was blood on the felt.

The first night I went for a drink in that pub a local guy guy came up to me and said, "Fight you for a pint, mate."
"No, it's ok," I said, "I'll buy you a pint, no need for a fight."
"No," said the local, "I want a pint for a fight."
"Look I'll buy you a pint if you want one."
"Bugger you," said the local. "I don't want your bloody pint," and he turned to the next guy at the bar who was another local. He laid him out with one punch.

I managed to do four months on this job without going insane, in fact I was feeling a lot better mentally. I came back to Fremantle having saved most of the money for the trip home but I wanted to save enough for a return trip in case of Jasia hating dear old England – you never know. Although immigrants are risking life and limb to get into the UK, it's not everyone's cup of tea. So I got myself two jobs, working on Fremantle Council, parks and gardens in the day and doing a cleaning job at night. For six months I did this, then we booked the tickets for England. We were to go on a package they had at the time called 'Ship Jet': you got a liner from Fremantle to Singapore, then a plane from there to Heathrow. The first part of the journey was great; you sailed to Singapore on this lovely passenger ship which took three days. Then you stayed on board in Singapore for three days before you got the flight to Heathrow. The only problem was when I tried to get off the boat in Singapore they wouldn't let me.

"What's the problem?" I asked the customs guy.
"Your hair's too long," he replied.
"You've got to be joking." But he wasn't.
At the time a bloke called Lee Kuan Yew governed Singapore. He had some very strange and strict rules in his country at the time, 1973. One of his rules was nobody could enter the country with hair that came over the

ears or down to the shoulder. So that ruled me out, as my hair at the time was shoulder length. His reasoning for this rule was that all foreigners with long hair were drug users or pushers. I suppose he had a point, but come on that's just generalising and stereotyping people. Another rule was that chewing gum was banned; you couldn't buy it or bring it into the country. I really wanted to go ashore and enjoy Singapore, after all we were there for three days and I didn't want to be stuck on the ship all that time. Someone suggested that I cut my hair. *No, why should I do that for some silly rule?* We got talking to this couple from Manchester who said that maybe I should wear a hat and tuck my hair under it. And that is what I did. We got a babysitter to look after Justin and we went ashore with this couple from Manchester. It was a lovely warm evening and the smells and atmosphere reminded me so much of Hong Kong. Someone on the boat suggested we take a walk down Boogie Street, as this was where the market and nightlife was.

As we walked down this street I Chinese guy approached us and said, "You want girls?"

"No thanks, as you can see we're with girls," I replied.

Not put off this guy says to the girls, "You want boys?"

"No thanks," Jasia said laughing.

This bloke wasn't giving up. "You want see blue movie? You want porn show? You like ping-pong?"

"No, we're ok," the Manchester lad told him.

"Then why you come down Boogie Street?" asked the hustler. I suppose he was right – it was a red light district. But we just wanted to people watch and have some fun.

Towards the end of a very enjoyable evening, I decided to let my hair down, literally. We were in a crowded bar and I took off my hat and shook my hair out. A huge cheer went up from all in the bar. Then a guy came up and warned me that if the city police see you with your long hair they will march you off to the barbers and cut it all off. So the hat went back on and we returned to the ship.

The flight home from Singapore was going to take 17 hours, and with a two and a half year old that was some task. As I said earlier, Justin has turned out to be a wonderful son and family man. But as a child he could be trying to say the least. It was probably our fault, we were a bit hippy-ish, in the sense that we would give him freedom to express himself and that's what he did. After all, who teaches you to be a parent? We were both very young and we hadn't done it before. As the plane took off everything was fine, and Justin was fast asleep. He looked quite angelic when he was asleep. There was a couple about our age sitting opposite us and saying how lovely Justin was and that they couldn't wait to have children and how lucky we were. That was before he woke up.

We had just started our lunch, and Justin was lying across my knee under the tray that drops down from the back of the seat. I had my meal on the tray; drinks, food. When Justin wakes up he doesn't come around slowly, he just springs up wide awake and ready to go. And that's just what he did, sprung up from under my tray like a Polaris missile, food, drinks, knives, forks; the whole shebang went flying through the air, most of it landing on the couple opposite. They were very understanding, *It's fine, don't worry about it, and he's only a baby.*

It would be non-stop for the next fifteen hours: my son had more energy than any Olympic athlete. By the time we reached Heathrow this couple were not talking to us and were probably put off kids for life.

You Never Said Goodbye

Dad as a young soldier

Me age 11 months with my Mum

John McArdle

Dad in background, Me as a soldier on Coronation day

My first pint with my Father in Hong Kong

You Never Said Goodbye

Dad, mum, Me, Coleen baby Rory and Sharon. Hong Kong 1958

Dad far left Mum centre, Hong Kong 1959

Homeland

I had been away from England for nearly five years. It was so strange to be back, like coming from a colour film to a black and white one. It was October, so everything was grey. It was 1973. It was the first time that Jasia had been to England. Her first impression was how close the houses were to one another. We had hired a car and drove up the M1-M6, so passing through Birmingham and Spaghetti Junction freaked her out, as she hadn't seen anything like it before. Everything is so spaced out in Australia and I don't mean that in the hippy sense. When we reached Liverpool I was a little nervous. I hadn't seen my mother, brothers and sisters for five years. I was also meeting Mum's new husband and daughter, my lovely half-sister Tricia.

I drove around the block a few times before I had the courage to stop outside the house. We got out of the car and the first one to greet us was Butch the family dog. He still remembered me after all those years. It was so great to see my mum and my brothers and sisters and meet my little sister Tricia. Everyone was bigger and older, they were so pleased to see me and meet my new family. Pat Mulvaney, my mum's new fella was very welcoming and friendly, but I didn't take to him. I don't know whether that was because he had taken your place dad, but my mother was happy with him and that was the main thing. They had a big welcome home party for us that night; my gran was there, aunties, uncles, cousins and friends. We sang old songs and I remember crying my eyes out when my mother sang. It brought back memories of when you and mum were together.

We stayed with my mum and Pat for a while until I found a job and somewhere to live. I got in touch with my half-brother, Chris, who was living in Rusden, Northamptonshire. He told me that there was lots of building work going on in that area and to get myself down there. He would put us up until we found a place of our own. So after five months back at home off we went. We stayed with Chris and his family for a few weeks then rented a place in Wellingborough. I landed myself a job as a scaffolder with one of the small firms in the area.

It was 1974 and there was plenty of building work in Northants, and the money was good so we had a decent standard of living. Two months into the job and I was promoted to Foreman Scaffolder. Not bad for a 24 year old. Because of my new position we were able to move into a new council house in Northampton. The house was on a new development on an estate called Thorplands. It was very nice; we had a three bed house with a man-made lake out the front and plenty of green land for the kids to play on. Jasia decided to enrol at the local college of further education to do some 'O' and 'A' levels. I worked lots of hours and enjoyed my job. I was in charge of about 15 men and I would allocate the jobs and oversee their work. This could be taxing sometimes, because scaffolders are hard-working guys but they're also hard drinking and tough men.

Jasia was enjoying her course at the college and made lots of new friends. Her new friends were people on her course but also some of the lecturers. She invited them for a meal one night and it was a real eye opener for me. I had never socialised with people like this before. They were middle-class, educated and had a different take on life to most of the people I knew. I always thought people like them were snobs and aloof. But I was wrong; they were really interesting, friendly and funny. And they were nearly all left-wingers. I've always had an inquisitive mind about the world around me and I found these people interesting. I always used to read the tabloids on a Sunday i.e. the *News of the*

World, *The Sunday Mirror*, etc. Jasia started getting the *Observer* and the *Guardian*, so I started to read them myself and found them much more informed as to what was going on at home and around the world.

When Jasia's friends from the college came around, I would feel left out sometimes because she had more in common with them. They would talk about art and politics and I was in the dark on both subjects. Jasia could tell this was a problem and suggested that I enrol on a part-time course at her college. She asked me what I wanted to do with my future. I thought about it and decided I would like to become a Safety Officer in the building industry. My goal would be to get 5 'O' levels, and then take an ONC at full time college to qualify. So at the age of 25, I enrolled for evening classes at the Northampton College of Further Education. It was hard work at first getting back into writing essays and doing research. I would get home from work at 5.30, have some food then out to college for 7, three nights a week. I was doing history, biology, art, maths and geography. I enjoyed all the subjects but maths. I always had a problem with numbers, and still do.

One day the lecturer from the drama department, Martin Banks approached me after one of my classes and asked for a favour. He had heard that I was a Scaffolder and wondered if I would build a set for their forthcoming production they were about to rehearse. I said of course I would, anything to help. They were doing a Tom Stoppard play called "Albert's Bridge". The studio was quite large and well equipped. The play was to be set in the round with a small bridge at one end, where a lot of the action was taking place. My job was to build that bridge out of Scaffolding and planks. Martin would rehearse the actors on the floor as I was in the background building the bridge. I was really interested in drama as I told you dad, and I'd really got into it just before I left school.

There was one actor in the company playing the part of a Northern industrialist and I didn't think he was getting it right, but who was I to judge? I was just the stagehand. Because this was a college production they had about 6 weeks of rehearsals, and on the third week of rehearsals the guy playing the industrialist had to drop out due to an illness. I overheard Martin and the class discussing who could take his place. They were scratching their heads and wondering who they could get at such short notice. When the rest of the group had gone, I approached Martin and asked if I could take over from the guy who had dropped out. He asked me what experience I had and I told him about my school plays ten years previously. Martin asked me to read for the part, which I did. He then announced to rest of the company that I was to play the industrialist. They were very surprised indeed – and so was I. The first night came very quickly and I was as nervous as hell. The play went well, I got good notices and people took an interest in me. Just like the school play, I was getting attention and I liked it. Martin asked me to join the drama group full time and without hesitation I accepted. Not only was I participating in drama, but I started to go to the theatre for the first time in my life.

We would get visiting fringe companies coming to the college and one of these companies influenced me greatly in becoming a professional actor later on. The name of that company was *7:84*, a political fringe touring company of a very high standard. Their founder was John McGrath, a playwright and dramatist. His actors take on multiple roles and frequently slip out of character in a Brecht style. His best known play is *The Cheviot, the Stag and the Black, Black Oil*, the title of the play referring to three pivotal periods in the history of class struggle in Scotland: the clearing of the Scottish Highlands to make way for grazing land, the subsequent use of land by the wealthy for shooting, and its current exploitation in the oil market. He had a pool of very talented performers that not only acted but were also fine musicians.

The play that I saw that changed my attitude towards theatre was called *Fish in the Sea*, about a group of factory workers in Merseyside occupying their factory to stop its closure. I found the play not only informative politically also very funny and a wonderful piece of theatre. That's when I made my mind up. *I want to be a professional actor. Where do I start?* I was now 25: *Am I too old? Am I good enough? How do I go about it?* Of course Martin was the one who would give me these answers. Martin was only a few years older than me and I liked his approach to theatre and his tastes. I had done a number of plays with him by now and attended a couple of drama festivals, so I felt confident enough to seek his advice. I told him I wanted to give up my job and become an actor full time, and how did I go about it?

"First of all," he said, "You have the talent and drive to do it." He said I was not too old as I had lots of life experience to bring to the table. He said most importantly, I should get the backing of my family and realise that I would have to give up a secure job for three years at college and at the end of it there would be no guarantee to work. It was a risk, but if I didn't take it I may regret it in the future.

I went home and discussed this life changing subject with Jasia. She was a hundred percent behind me.

"Go follow your dream," she said. "You have a talent - don't waste it."

So the plan was that I would apply for drama schools in the autumn, but as an alternative if I didn't get into any of the drama schools I would also apply for polytechnic to become a Safety Officer. Martin and his assistant helped me choose my audition pieces. For most drama schools at the time you had to prepare three speeches of at least three minutes long. One had to be a Shakespeare, one modern and one of your own choice. So we came up with 'Thou Nature', the Edmond speech from *King Lear* for the Shakespeare, the toilet speech from a play by Ted Whitehead called *The Foursome* and a speech where Peer Gynt lies to his mother. Three very different speeches. I worked on the speeches for a couple of weeks with Martin and when I was ready I applied to some drama schools. First on my list was E15 in Loughton in Essex, then Central School of Speech and Drama, RADA, and an outsider Birmingham University.

The first place I auditioned was Birmingham. I drove to Birmingham on the day, as it's not that far from Northampton. When I got there, two people were waiting to go in and one was on her way out.

'How did it go?' I asked.

'Fine. They're really friendly, no need to worry," the girl said, and went out the door.

That was good news but it was still nerve wracking waiting to go in. My turn came and in I went.

It was quite a large room with a table at one end, with three people sitting behind it: a young woman, who smiled, a middle-aged man with a bald head, who did not smile and an older woman who looked quite frightening. I had to give my name and then start my speeches. I did the Shakespeare first, that didn't go too bad – I forgot a bit in the middle but carried on. Then my modern speech, which was quite shocking, because it contained some swearing and sexual descriptions. The three behind the desk didn't look that impressed so I had to do something spectacular for my Peer Gynt. This speech I made more physical, jumping up onto their desk and sitting on the chair and running around the room. This seemed to wake them up. After I had finished they thanked me and said they would be in touch. Two days later they offered me a place on their course. What a confidence booster – my first audition and I had been offered a place.

The next place I auditioned was E15. One of the reasons I had chosen this school was a good friend of mine Peter Dykstra had been there a year and highly recommended it. It was a drama school that used the 'method' which is an approach to acting used by many great American actors of the 50s and 60s, actors such as Marlon Brando and James Dean. It was based on Stanislavski, a Russian dramatist from the Moscow arts theatre in 1911. His technique was used to train actors to draw believable emotions to their performances. This type of acting philosophy appealed to me, as it was more from the gut, a more emotional and natural way of conveying the character. To get to E15 acting school I had to get a train from

John McArdle

Northampton to Euston, then catch a tube on the central line to Debden, then a quarter of a mile walk to the school. I walked up the long drive to E15 and I knew straight away: this was where I wanted to be. The surroundings impressed me at first sight. You walked along a short driveway to the main house, which was a huge beautiful Georgian building with a pond in front. This is where the main acting classes were held and where I had to report to. I was directed to the Barn Theatre, which was across from the main house in the grounds. This theatre barn had a foyer with a bar and seating area, where all the auditionees were gathered.

There was an eclectic mix in terms of race, age and class types. Most of them were younger than me; I was 27 by now and the average age here was 20. This was a completely different type of audition to Birmingham. The tutors, a woman called Janet Nelson and an Australian man called Janis Balotis, split us up into two groups. I was on Janet's team. She had us do a series of games to help us loosen up and to get to know the other people that we were auditioning with. We spent about an hour doing that and then we did some vocal exercises. It was great; it was like a mini workshop to warm you up before you did your audition speeches. We had lunch and by now I had made a few friends. It was very relaxing, a perfect way to begin what is usually a nerve wracking process.

After lunch we started the speeches. It was not like in Birmingham where you went in one at a time. We all went into the main theatre together. It was interesting watching the others do their speeches; it helped you gauge your own work. Some were awful and didn't seem to have a clue and others where frighteningly good.

My turn came and Janet said, "Ok, John give us your first speech."
"Which one?" I asked.
"Any," replied Janis.
So I started with the Edmund speech from King Lear. I was doing it very traditionally, RP.

Janet stopped me halfway through and said, "Where are you from originally?"

"Liverpool," I replied.

"Well do the speech in a Liverpool accent then. And give him something to do, don't just stand there."

So I gave myself a minute to think about it, then re started the speech. I played Edmund with a Scouse accent, having a shave in front of a mirror. They let me finish the whole speech, and then Janis asked me about the character. *What was his situation during that speech, what were his feelings?* Luckily I had read the whole play so I knew all about him; I even put in some of my own made up thoughts about the character. I did my other two speeches and then we went outside to do some improvisation. Now it got a little scary, for outside were some of the 2nd and 3rd year students, watching and participating. Janet asked me to do my Edmund speech again in a Liverpool accent. I had been happy doing it in the theatre but out here with the other students it was a little more intimidating.

I had just started, when one of the students interrupted me.

"What the fuck do you think you're doing?" he said.

I carried on trying to ignore him, but he carried on interrupting me, saying, "You can't act. You're fuckin useless."

I stopped the speech, grabbed this guy by his lapels and said, "You carry on doing this and you won't be able to talk anymore," staying in character.

He backed off very quickly, saying, "Sorry mate, it's only a game".

I noticed Janet and Janis were trying not to laugh.

When we had finished the tutors told us to stay around for the rest of the day to explore the school. It was a lovely day and the whole school seemed to be outside. My friend Peter Dykstra was doing a play on the lawn; I think it was a Chekhov and all the actors were dressed in period costumes. Dykstra came off the acting area and found this big truck tyre, he picked it up then rolled it into the acting area. It rolled right into the middle of a couple having a dialogue, they didn't even flinch, they just carried on the scene. I asked later why he did that. *To test their concentration*, he said. At the end of the day I went away buzzing. That was where I wanted to go, there was no doubt. But would I get in? It was now a waiting game.

It took a week for the letter to come. I opened the letter and they had offered me a place on their three-year acting course, subject to grants. I was over the bloody moon; I had been accepted at one of the best drama schools in London. My life was about to change. I didn't even bother doing my RADA and Central auditions. I was going where I wanted to be.

My next step was to apply for a grant. I filled in all the forms to apply for maintenance grant and fees. But there was a problem over the grant for my fees, which at the time were £3,000, a lot of money in the seventies. My local authorities had turned down my application for the grant fees on the grounds that it was a non-vocational course. The maintenance grant was fine because I had been working for the past 10 years and paying taxes but they would not honour the course fee. This was a huge blow. My dreams were shattered. I couldn't afford to pay the fees myself – it was too expensive. I wrote to my local authorities begging them to change their minds but to no avail. I wrote to various charities asking for their help, but had no luck there. I could have accepted the Birmingham offer because it was a degree course, but I didn't want to go there as my heart was set on E15. At the same time I had also been offered a place at Nottingham Polytechnic to become a safety officer. It was decision time: what should I do? Go to Birmingham and do a degree in Performing Arts or take the more secure option and go to Nottingham?

I wrote to E15 informing them I couldn't take the offer due to grant issues relating to the fees. Three days after I sent the letter, I received a reply from them. They said I could come to some arrangement with the school to pay for my fees. I could either get a part-time job outside the school and pay off the fees or I could do some cleaning in the school and pay them off that way. This was brilliant – I could go to E15 after all. It would be hard work but worth it in the long run.

It was now November 1976 and the first term started late September 1977 so I had ten months to save some money and prepare for drama school. I worked hard during that time, working long hours and reading up on plays and theatre. Jasia and I hardly saw each other, she was busy with her studies in art and history, and I think we were beginning to drift apart even before I left for drama school. I know I sound selfish doing this while having the responsibility of a family, but I was the eldest of five children and had spent a lot of my early life looking after my brothers and sisters. When I left school at 15 I only had six years of independence and then I was a father. I felt I needed to do this. After all, in the back of my mind I was going to die at 48, because of your early death – I thought it was hereditary.

In my mind I only had 20 years to make my mark in life. I knew I was going to miss Justin and I loved him dearly. He was eight now with a vivid imagination.

He had a new teacher at his school and we had never met her.

I asked him, "What is she like?"

He replied, "In fact, Dad, she is the Queen of England."

"Is she really?" I said, naturally not believing him!

On the school open day we met her. He wasn't far wrong - she was the image of Queen Elizabeth and she even sounded like her.

On another occasion we had got a babysitter to look after Justin whilst we went out for the evening. When we arrived home at around midnight, there was a police car outside the house. We thought my God what's happened? The babysitter was in tears.

"He's gone," she said. "I went to check on him an hour ago and he wasn't in his bed."

Because of the commotion the next door neighbours came out to see what was going on. When we told them they said, "He's in our house with us."

What had happened was that Justin had woken up, walked out of the front door without the babysitter knowing, gone next door and told them that his Mummy and Daddy had left him on his own! Never a dull moment.

My True Beginning

The time was getting near to start drama school. I was going to have to find some accommodation and that was going to be expensive. If I was going to pay rent anywhere near the school it would cost me a fortune and eat up most of my maintenance grant, so I had to think of a cheaper way. I came up with what I thought was a brilliant idea. A guy I knew was selling his ex-ambulance that he had converted into a camper van. It was ideal. It had a bunk bed, a fridge, a stereo system and an oven. Everything I needed, it would also serve as my transport to get around. This investment would save me a fortune in rent. All I needed was a site, but I would sort that problem out when I got there.

The time came and I set off for Loughton, Essex. It was about 68 miles, so I could even come home when I had weekends off. I was excited and nervous about starting drama school; after all it was a life-changing decision. I arrived in the large car park at E15 and decided there was plenty of room to park my ambulance there. The first day was all about registering and getting to know the other people in your year. Right from the start I loved it. I was getting a grant to do what I really wanted to do in life. At the end of the first day we all went for a drink in the foyer and then everyone went to his or her new homes. I of course went to my lonely camper van. In fact it was very cosy. I had a few beers in the fridge, made something nice for dinner, played some chilled out music on the sound system and opened the doors of the van to let in the early autumn smells and sunset. I had no neighbours as the E15 car park was surrounded by trees and bushes and was not visible from the road – it was perfect. The only downer was I had to get up at 6am to start my cleaning job in the school. My duties before lessons were to clean and hoover the main house and toilets and after lessons in the evening to clean the theatre foyer and theatre. So I had a long day, say from 6am to 7pm but I knew it would be worth it.

On the second day we had singing lessons led by Michael Rowland, a really committed teacher especially if you were a good singer, which I was not. I still enjoyed it immensely. We would sing mainly ensemble pieces such as *Carmina Burana* and some Gilbert and Sullivan classics. It was great fun, and at the end of term we would perform one of the operas to the rest of the school. Later we had movement with a wonderful tutor called Jo Jelly. She showed us how to move with ease and confidence on stage and also how to relax and be free from nerves before a performance. She also introduced me to the music of Tom Waits; she would play some of his music during relaxation after a vigorous workout. I was learning so much very quickly about music, self-awareness, art, books, history, people and felt so privileged to be there. Then we had what we were here for: acting lessons. It was not so much teaching you how to act but to hone the talent that you had to make your performance real, naturalistic and honest. Janis and Janet usually took these classes, as they were our year tutors. I loved these lessons; I learnt so much about my strengths and weaknesses as an actor. I started to make new friends and soon sussed out who was good and who I wanted to work with. I made one particular friend, who is still a really good mate after 32 years: Seamus O'Neill.

Seamus and I got on from the start; we were of a similar age and background. He came from an army family and had travelled around a lot. He had been in Germany for many years and he speaks the language fluently. Seamus and I would have some great fun together during our time at E15. Every Friday you had a task called 'Entertainment' You had to come up with something to entertain the rest of your year; you could do anything you wanted as long as it was entertaining! It was a bit like 'Britain's Got

Talent' It got harder and harder as the term went on trying to come up with something original every week. You also had to fit this in between your normal lessons. I remember one Friday, Seamus and I had nothing prepared for the entertainment. We had left it too late – it was 4.30 and the entertainments started at 5. What were we going to do? Then Seamus came up with this brilliant idea.

"Let's do 'The Bin Man Song'"

'What's 'The Bin Man Song?' said I

Seamus explained. He would step inside a metal dustbin, holding the handles either side and hop about. I would slip my feet into two metal dustbin lids and my hands into two others, clanging and bashing about singing what turned out to be an improvised song 'We are the Dustbin Men'. Considering it was a rushed job, it went down a treat. People were falling about laughing. Janis and Janet just looked at each other with a knowing look: we had just about got away with it but you couldn't say it wasn't different!

There was so much we had to learn to become accomplished stage actors. Stage fighting was one of my favourite lessons. We had a big butch tutor that looked like Pluto out of Popeye, and the students named him Phil the Fence. We learnt about all the historical methods of sword and axe fighting from the Roman gladiators to the duellists of 18th century Europe. After the 2nd year you could take your stage-fighting certificate, which would entitle you to instruct stage fighting at a basic level.

One of the most important classes was of course 'Voice' as this is your most important instrument as an actor. To be able to use your voice properly on stage is vital. You learn how to project without straining the vocal cords. If you are on stage six days a week performing eight shows you need know how to breathe and project your voice with confidence and ease. Part of the voice training was to try to lose your accent when needed. If you had a regional accent you could be stuck in a pigeon hole and only play parts associated with your background. But if you could master Received

Pronunciation, you would have a wider range of parts to play. All the technical training was so important to improve your skill as a professional actor. I was never bored with any of this work, I was so happy to be where I was and what I was doing.

But at the end of each day when everyone had gone to their shared flats and houses, I would continue to do my cleaning work until 7pm and then back to my little camper van. One night I decided to have a bit of a party in my camper. I invited about 20 people, cooked burgers and sausages and everyone brought booze. We had a great time but unfortunately the school had a few complaints from nearby residents and that was the end of my parking at the college. I had to find some other place to park up each night. I tried to park up in Epping Forest but after a while the police told me it was illegal and I had to move on. I felt a bit like a lone gypsy. Also the vehicle itself started to break down a lot, in fact I was on first name terms with most of the RAC men. I had to get rid of the ambulance – it was costing me too much money. So I sold it and bought a Morris Minor, a great little car.

Now I had nowhere to live and I couldn't afford rent. My friend Peter Dykstra was living in a squat with his Israeli girlfriend and her daughter. He said that I could join them for the princely sum of £5 a week. How could I refuse? The squat was a vicarage about 1 mile from the school. They occupied the ground floor and said I could have any room I that I liked on the first floor. It was totally unfurnished so I had no bed, wardrobe or cupboards. I picked the room with the least damage but even this had gothic windows with a two inch gap between the frame and the walls and in winter there was a low mist in the room. I used to sleep on the floor in a sleeping bag and I would wake up with mice running past my head. It was almost free though, so I couldn't complain. In the second year I bought a second-hand bed – luxury!

Peter's girlfriend Ruth was an attractive 23year old ex-Israeli soldier who had a three year old daughter called Luna, from a previous relationship. Luna would go to nursery when Ruth was at college and sometimes I would run them to nursery because they had no transport. In fact Ruth said I *should* do this as they had done me a favour letting me stay in their squat, so I had no choice – another job before college. She was a very strong woman and I named her the 'Israeli Tank Commander' but of course I never told her!!

Peter and Ruth were in their second year so they were on a more advanced stage of the course that included improvisation and in depth character study. I was woken one morning at about 2am as I could hear shouting coming from downstairs. It sounded like a really bad row going on and as it got more and more intense I could hear smashing of plates and glasses. I would have gone down sooner if Luna had been at home but she was away for the week with her grandparents. Then I heard crying and screaming. That was it, I couldn't just lie there and listen to Ruth getting beaten up, I had to do something, I had to interfere.

So I went downstairs and flung the door open and shouted, "What the fuck's going on?"

They were standing on the bed both half naked, Peter with blood streaming down his head and Ruth with a bottle in her hand. They stopped what they were doing and Peter said, "We were in the middle of an improvisation."

I shut the door and went back to bed thinking 'Bloody Hell is this what you have to do to be an actor!?'

I was now reaching the end of my first year and our final project was a full scale re-enactment of an historical event. Our year had to pick an event in history that we could re-enact and produce for a full week. The first part was finding something that involved the whole year. We decided on the immigration of people from England to the Canadian Prairies in 1828. Then we had to research what sort of people set out on this arduous journey, what kind of transport they used when they reached Canada and their day-to-day lives on the journey from Halifax to Saskatchewan. We then each had to decide which character we were to portray on this journey and stay in that character for a whole week. Some of the students formed themselves into families, others were couples. Seamus and I decided on being a pair of Irish tinkers, with only ourselves to look after. These projects became known as 'The Trek'. We were going to do it over a week and even camp out for a couple of nights in Epping Forest.

The time came and we set of in this long procession of people dressed in 18th-century clothing pulling handcarts and trying to ignore the traffic. We passed through Debden on the way to Epping Forest, but the general public didn't turn a hair. I think they were so used to having a bunch of crazy drama school students among them each day they were used to it. We reached the forest and made camp. Of course Seamus and I had not come prepared with food and drink, so we had to scrounge off the other trekkers. This was all in character of course as the two Irish men would not have had any money so we were only being honest to our characters! Anyway we helped the others to light fires and cook so we were of service.

It was very hard to stay in character and ignore the modern world around you. One day Seamus and I were walking along the path in the forest and a jumbo jet was flying above us.

Seamus looked up and said, "What the hell is that?"

"It looks like an iron bird to me," I said.

It was tough going keeping this up for a week but good fun too. We got to the end and had a great celebration. You really do miss life's little luxuries, even if it was for only a week. We were coming to the end of my first year at drama school and I felt that I had learned such a lot in a short time. I said my goodbyes to everyone and headed home.

My marriage was sadly coming to an end. We both knew it was a lost cause but thought we could try a little harder for the sake of Justin. I got some work in a tannery for a couple of weeks. It was a horrible smelly job. This made me even more determined to become a professional actor. I started to get a copy of *The Stage*; this is a weekly journal for all up and coming actors. It was full of revues from reps all over the country; it also advertised auditions for fringe companies. I gave myself a goal: that

I would apply for an audition for one of these fringe jobs and if I got it I would be paid for something I was being trained for. So I wrote off to a company called 'Reflex Action Theatre Company', who were holding auditions in London. I didn't tell them I was still at drama school because I never thought I had a cat in hells chance of getting the job. They offered me an audition the following week.

The meetings were held in an old church off the Tottenham Court Road. When I got there it was full of very confident young actors and actresses, about 40 people altogether. After we had done our speeches it was whittled down to about twenty people. After lunch we did group games and improvisations. We also did some physical workouts because the director Dafydd Hughes believed in his actors being fit. At the end of the day, the director called out the names of four girls and four guys to come back tomorrow to be considered for the two places available and mine was one of them. I was over the moon: my very first audition and I had made it down to the last four out of 40 people. I came back the next day hoping to get my first paid acting work.

It was hard going competing against such talented opposition. We finished the final audition at about 4pm; I was drained mentally and physically. Dafydd said he would let us know the next day. The day came and the phone rang. That's the main issue about being an actor: the phone ringing. Even if you're in work when you hear that phone ringing you want it to be your agent with the offer of more work. The phone rang and it was Dafydd, saying he would like to offer me the job. A six week contract, starting in a week, in Cardiff at the Sherman Theatre and the money was £68 a week plus subsistence. I didn't listen to the deal; all I heard was the word 'offer'. Yes of course I would accept. I put the phone down and started punching the air: *I've landed my first pro job and I am still at drama school!!*

But taking this job meant I would miss the first three weeks of my second year at drama school, so I had to get their permission. That wasn't easy because Margaret Bury, the Principal of E15 didn't like her students going off and getting jobs before they had finished their courses. She did give me her blessing, even if it was with a warning not to make it a habit.

I was contracted to do a play called *The Dream of Reason*. It was a two-hander about Anton Mesmer, the father of hypnotism and was set during the Renaissance period in Paris. I was to play Anton Mesmer and another actor called Simon was to play a number of roles within the play. It was a very physical piece so we used to do two-hour warm-ups before we rehearsed. I found the rehearsals hard-going, as not only did we work on the play, but we also had to do intense research into that period of history. So there was lots of reading to do besides learning your lines. I also had to learn to play the glass harmonica, because Mesmer used to play it in his salons during his hypnosis sessions. The glass harmonica was a mixture of wine glasses of different shapes and sizes and different levels of water in them. You would wet your index fingers and move them round the rims of the glasses thus making a high-pitched sound that was beautiful and musical. Mozart even wrote a piece for Mesmer that included the glass harmonica. This was all hard work but I loved every minute of it. We would start work at 10am until about 6pm then back to my digs to learn lines and background reading until midnight. As we had only three and a half weeks rehearsal we had to cram it all in.

It was getting near to the first performance and I was getting more nervous the closer we got. After all, it was my very first professional job as an actor. The opening night came and we had to go on stage in the round, just the two of us for the next two hours and I was shaking like mad. I was thinking, *I can't do this, there is so much to remember.* The lights went down and we walked on to the stage - there was no going back. I lost all nervousness as soon as I did my first speech and the play moved along so fast it was all over before I knew it. The audience seemed to love it; I think we took three curtain calls. Dafydd was also pleased; all our hard work had paid off. The reviews in the press the next day were nearly all favourable and I along with my fellow actor got good notices on our performances. I was a happy man. Dafydd thought that Simon and I worked well together and that we should do some live improvisational shows in the Sherman theatre where we were performing *Mesmer*. So in the day we would work on some structure behind the improvisation shows with the idea of performing them on Friday and Saturdays after our main show. The audience could buy an extra ticket to stay behind for the improv show. On our first performance the audience went mad – they loved it. And so did we. It was fun to do, no lines to learn, all you had to do was use your imagination and acting skills. We also had a new cast member for the improv shows. His name was Joe Leeway, who later found fame as a member of the eighties pop group The Thompson Twins.

I liked Cardiff. The people were friendly and there were lots of good pubs and clubs to go to. We used to rehearse in a place called the Chapter Arts Centre in Canton and this is where all the arty people hung out. They had a cinema for arthouse films, a theatre for visiting fringe companies and a healthy eating restaurant. I spent a happy eight weeks doing this job but sadly it had come to an end. We had a big wrap party and Dafydd said I could come back and work for him anytime. This was so encouraging and gave me more confidence to return to drama school with a small taste of professional theatre experience.

Love of my Life

It was 1978 and the punk era was popular. I bought my first punk album 'New Boots and Panties' by Ian Drury and I had my hair cut a bit spiky but didn't go the whole punk hog, safety pins and all that. I was into some of the music, though after all I was getting on a bit now. I was 28.

I went back to Northampton to see my son Justin and talk to Jasia about the future of our relationship. It didn't look to good, I'm afraid. We had got married too young and had drifted apart doing our own things. It was sad for us but it was even sadder for Justin.

I returned to drama school three weeks late because of my job, so I had a lot of catching up to do. It was great to see all the people I had worked with last year, although not all of them had returned. We started with around 40 in the first year and now it had been slimmed down to twenty. Some had left of their own accord and some had not been asked back. The second year became a bit more serious. We would be doing full-length plays and most of them would be the classics. We would be performing and studying Shakespeare, Ibsen, Steinberg, Tennessee Williams and Chekhov.

One of the lessons I really enjoyed was gymnastics. It was because of you, Dad – all that sport and training you pushed me to do was now second nature, and gymnastics would prove important in the early part of my career. We had gym on a Thursday, after the first years had their lesson. I was now a second year and this made a big difference when it came to talking to the first year students; they looked up to you and made you feel important.

So we headed into the gym just as the first years where finishing off their session. Seamus and I were checking out the new talent and my eyes were drawn to a really beautiful young girl in a light blue leotard that matched her beautiful eyes. She also had on blue leg warmers and gave me the nicest smile. We just nodded hello to each other and I went off to get changed. I was still married, just about, and though technically separated I was not ready to jump into a new relationship. So I put it out of my mind. I must get on with my training as an actor and not get distracted. Still in the back of my mind I knew this girl I had just seen could be a big distraction. I had to be strong.

E15 was a drama school that took risks and that's what I liked about it, but one risk went a bit too far for my liking. Our year tutor at the time was a really good actress called Kate Williams. She was on television and famous for a sitcom she had been in from the early seventies, called *Love Thy Neighbour*. Kate was teaching us the Master and Servant lessons. The reason behind these lessons were related to the plays we were about to embark on. Most of these plays would have kings and queens and their servants or industrialists and their workers. So it was to define the characters between the classes and their attitudes to one another. One way of illustrating this was using playing cards. You would shuffle the playing cards and lay them on the table; you would then pick a card. If you picked a king or queen you would act accordingly and if you picked an ace or low card that would also depict your status. You then acted out through improvisation what level you had picked, and then the other members of the class had to guess what your status was: upper, middle or lower. There were various other exercises to achieve this master-servant relationship.

One however proved to go a bit too far. One day we had a visiting tutor who divided the class into two groups and said that one group would represent the Nazi SS in control of a concentration camp during WW2 and the other group would be the inmates of the camp. This tutor seemed to have picked nice easy-going people to represent the SS and more aggressive confident students to represent the Jewish inmates. The scenario was: a new batch of inmates had arrived in Auschwitz and the Gestapo had to process them. I was picked to be a member of the SS. We started off aggressively herding the other group in to a large room in the main house of the school. We made them move all of the furniture out of the room. We then lined them up and asked them to take off all their jewellery and place it in a box, and then we made them do really hard physical tasks like running up and down the stairs non-stop for about 20 minutes. From the start of this exercise we shouted at them non-stop and if they answered us back we made them do 50 press-ups or run up the stairs again. All this was bad enough, and I was actually feeling terrible while I was doing this, but tried to convince myself that it was all part of staying in character and being able to cope with an uncomfortable situation. But some of our group seemed to be getting off on this power and things got worse. One of our group told them all to strip off naked, and without hesitation they did. They actually looked terrified. They were then told to go outside the house and run naked through the school grounds which they did. It was November and there was snow on the ground, so they must have been freezing. They were then ushered back into the house and some of them were in tears and really shaken up. I realised the some of the class were actually Jewish so it must have been especially hard for them.

Once back in the house they were split into groups and our group was making them do humiliating things to each other. I noticed one group had a beautiful Californian girl spread eagled on the floor and a guy was undoing his trousers. That was it - I had to intervene.

"What the hell do you think you're doing?" I said to bloke undoing his trousers.

"What does it look like?" he replied.

I grabbed him and pushed him away from the girl. I was then backed up by a very lovely man called James Ray Smith.
He said, "Things are getting out of hand and we need to stop this right now."
We were told to leave the room, which we did, but soon after the exercise was stopped.

I think improvisation and character experience is important to acting but there should be limits. It's not real life. This sort of exercise could cause damage and psychological games could be dangerous. It was not all like this, but every now and again something controversial would happen – it was that sort of drama school.

I was enjoying the second year. We were doing actual full-length plays as opposed to scenes from plays like we'd done in our first year. I was cast as Doctor Wangel in Ibsen's play *Lady from the Sea*. It was the first time on stage that I 'went through the mirror'. This means I was at one with myself and the character and I was fully concentrated on being in the now as Dr Wangel. I used my 'emotional springboard' to make Dr Wangel cry in the final scene. An emotional springboard is using something from your past that has upset you and putting it into the scene you are playing to get the same effect. In this case I used you, Dad, the day you left us. In the next play I found that I could do comedy, through playing a character. The play was *Heartbreak House* by George Bernard Shaw, and the part I played was Mazzini Dunn.

It was getting close to Christmas so the first years were preparing their entertainments for the Christmas party. We didn't need to do it in our year but if they needed any help then we would oblige. One of our year students, Martin Pallet, was devising something with some of the first years and asked me if I wanted to be involved.
"Who else is doing it?" I asked.

When he told me that Kathy, the girl I'd met in the gym at the beginning of the year was in it I didn't hesitate. I just said yes. It was an acapella song, *Gaude te*, very Christmassy medieval folk song. I am an average singer, not really West End material, but this Kathy Pickard had the most wonderful voice. She was a natural singer of a high standard. She also had this lovely accent, proper northern. On top of all that she was beautiful and intelligent. What more could a man ask for? But I had to stay strong, as I was going through the end of a long relationship and I didn't want to complicate things. That didn't stop me flirting with her though. I think Martin Pallet was a bit pissed off, because he had his eye on her too.

We would rehearse every night after lessons and I was getting to fancy Kathy more and more. She had a great sense of humour and we got on very well. It was the last day of term before the Christmas break and we were to perform our entertainment for the college. It went really well and we all stayed behind for the party. Towards the end of the night I was talking to Kathy on her own in a corner of the theatre, and I just kissed her and then asked her if she would go out with me. To my delight she said yes. We had a wonderful evening together and said we would see each other after the Christmas break.

I spent Christmas in Northampton with my son Justin. I had missed not seeing him every day and felt guilt-ridden at the time. After all it's not a child's fault that his parents are splitting up, and it's hard for them to understand. They just want you to be together. I loved Justin very much and it was breaking my heart. I tried to see him as often as I could, but because of the distance and the work I had to do it was not that often. Sometimes I'd wonder if I'd done the right thing. I had lost my marriage, my home, a secure job and most of all my son. I had no money and really nowhere to live. I was still living in the squat that had no heating and no window in my bedroom. I must have been mad. But it was no use living a lie and Jasia and I sadly couldn't make our marriage work. I knew what it was like to lose you dad and in a way I was deliberately leaving him without a father. Obviously I would still be in his life but it wouldn't be the same. It was a sad and difficult time for all of us but especially Justin.

I went back to college after Christmas and eventually started to see Kathy. We went out for about three months and then I decided that we should finish our relationship. She was only young, 21, and we would be starting out as actors soon and probably be working at different ends of the country from one another. Why fall in love for it all to go wrong after we start our professional careers? I think I was still struggling with the breakup of my marriage and leaving Justin. Perhaps it was all too soon. So we decided to finish the relationship. We still saw each other every day at college and we still felt the same about each other, so it wasn't long before we decided to get back together and see how it went.

We were getting towards the end of my second year and I was approached by a company in Cardiff to do a new devised play that would take me right through the summer. This meant that I would miss at least four weeks of my first term in my third year. Again I had to ask permission from the principle Margaret Bury. She said there was no way that I could miss that much work at the beginning of my third year. I had to make up my mind what I wanted to do, take this paid acting job or stay on for another year at drama school. I was 28 now, so I wanted to get out in the professional world of acting sooner rather than later. I discussed this with Kathy and she said it was my decision and would stand by me no matter what, even though she would miss me (she still had another two years left at college). I decided to take the job and take my chances out there in the real world of Acting.

The company I would be working for was mainly actors from Iceland, a real mad bunch of crazy, lovely actors. We were to devise a show in four weeks and then perform it in the community of Cardiff for six weeks. Kathy came to join me for the summer, so everything was working out fine. We found some nice digs just outside Cardiff in a place called Llandaff. We had a bedsit but with a little kitchenette. Kathy found a job in the day behind the bar at a pub near the Cardiff Arms Park. She had to pull the pints just right for the old timers, with just the right head or they'd make her pour it away and start again. She didn't last long as they were wasting too much beer! Justin came up to join us for 3 weeks and I had to introduce him to Kathy. He didn't like her one bit. After all this was not his mum and he must have felt threatened by this stranger in her place. It was also hard for Kathy; she was young and had no experience with 8 year-old boys. Still we got through it and we hoped things would improve.

One night in the digs Kathy and I were watching *Hammer House of Horror*, a Dracula film, which was very scary. During the commercial break Kathy went to make some tea. While she was in the kitchen I got out a set of vampire teeth that I had bought for Justin that he had left behind. What a great opportunity to play a trick on Kathy when she came back in. I slipped the very real-looking vampire teeth into my mouth.

Kathy came back into the room with a tray of tea and biscuits and on cue she said, "Do you really think there are such things as vampires?"

I just smiled showing my perfect set of vampire teeth. Kathy screamed, dropped the tray and ran out of the flat. We laughed about it afterwards, when I'd managed to calm her down but the joke backfired on me later – I woke up screaming after a horrible nightmare about vampires.

The summer soon came to an end. Kathy had to go back to E15 and I would soon be finishing this job and be out of work. Kathy lived in Buckhurst Hill, sharing a flat with 4 other students from E15; she said I could move in with her, because I had nowhere to live. Kathy went back to college to start her second year and I got out *The Stage* to look for work. I really needed a job with an Equity Card because in those days you couldn't call yourself a professional actor without one. It was a bit of a catch 22; you had to have an Equity Card to work in Repertory Theatre and the West End but you couldn't get a job without one. Many theatre companies were allocated about five cards a year to give to new members. They were much sought after and like gold dust. Auditions that advertised a job with an Equity Card were inundated with applicants so it was difficult obtaining one.

There was an ad in the Stage for an actor/musician to join a theatre company called 'Stirabout' run by its founder Corrina Seeds. This was a company that toured British borstals and prisons with comedy sketches and music, and it came with an Equity Card. I applied, even though the only instrument I could play was a blues harmonica, and I could only play by ear and improvisation. I went along to the audition and did my speeches and improvisation, which went well. Then it came to my music audition. Other applicants played guitar, saxophone, piano, flute and percussion and they were good. It then came my turn to show my musical prowess. It looked at first glance like I had no instrument to play, and then out of my pocket I produced my little blues harp.

The director of Stirabout, Corrina Seeds said, "Ok, John, what are you going to play for us?'

I had to think on my feet so I said it's a number called 'The Memphis Train' something I was going to make up on the spot. I started off real slow, like a train pulling out from a station, and then gradually got faster and faster. They seemed to like what I was doing because they were all clapping along. I went away feeling I had done my best, so it was up to them. I had no agent at the time so I left them my phone number at Kathy's house. When I got home later that day Kathy said they had phoned from Stirabout and would I call them back. I called them and Corrina offered me a nine-month contract with an Equity Card. I had done it! I would now be a Professional Actor and there was no going back to scaffolding. I made myself a promise that once I started as a professional actor I would do nothing else, not even work behind a bar or drive a taxi, if I didn't make my living as an actor I would just starve.

More Porridge

I would be working with a very talented group, Gary, who sang and played guitar, Simon who also played guitar,
Maureen, a very funny actress with a lovely singing voice, and Marianne, who played the flute. We rehearsed in Chalk Farm for 6 weeks so I was able to go home to Kathy every night, which was a good start. Once the rehearsals were finished we would then be on tour of the country for the next seven months. We did most of the big maximum security prisons: Wormwood Scrubs, Holloway, Long Lartin, and Brixton. We also did shows in open prisons like Ford and Leyhill. It was interesting playing to a captive audience, if they didn't like you they would let you know, after all most of these guys on the outside went to clubs with good singers and comics, so they wouldn't settle for any old rubbish.

I remember once we were doing a show at Long Lartin Maximum Security Prison in the heart of Worcestershire. This prison housed some of the country's most dangerous prisoners. Armed robbers, Palestinian terrorists, and murderers and rapists. So they weren't going to be a pleasant audience. The first thing we noticed when we entered the prison was that there were no keys. We were accompanied to the hall by one of the wardens who would enter a code into a computer to open the doors. There were cameras everywhere, this was one very secure prison. The joke was that although we were playing to a captive audience if the prisoners didn't want to come they wouldn't. Most of them came along though, if only to get out of their cell and ogle the pretty actresses. We put the portable set up in the main hall and went back to a secure room to get ready.

The evening started well. We did a sketch about a bank robbery, written by Spike Milligan, and that went down well. I always played the baddie in these sketches so the inmates always cheered me on. There was an audience of about 350 prisoners and the guys on the front row looked like extras from *The Sopranos*. Simon had a monologue half way through the evening, by Peter Cook, called 'I would rather be a judge than a miner'. Now this monologue was taking the piss out of judges but you only realised that after a few lines into the speech. On stage there would be just a single chair and a spotlight on it. Simon, dressed in a judge's wig and gown, would walk to the chair and start the monologue.

We were backstage getting ready for the next set. As soon as Simon walked out, we heard what sounded like the tubular chairs the prisoners were sitting on rattling. This sound got louder and louder, and then some members of our audience started to shout abuse at Simon. I peeked my head round the curtain and I could see the guys on the front row making cutthroat gestures to Simon. Then one of the chairs was thrown onto the stage. The lights went up and prison officers appeared from nowhere with batons and helmets. The officer who was looking after us rushed us all into a cell for our own protection; poor Simon was as white as a sheet. The prisoners where all corralled back to the cells without too much damage to property or life. As soon as Simon had appeared onstage dressed as a judge it was like a red rag to a bull. Most of the guys in this prison were in for life and the person that gave them that sentence was a judge. In hindsight it wasn't the best idea to include it in the programme! It also brought back unhappy memories for me even though I had only done a three-month sentence in New Zealand.

I found the women's prisons harder than the men's. In the men's prisons they wouldn't usually shout out rude things to the girls on stage, they had this sort of code of conduct and they didn't want to be associated with sex offenders. On the other hand the women didn't give a damn, they shouted stuff all the time to us lads: *Get em off* and *Do you fancy a shag?* It could be quite scary but great audiences and a bit like adult pantomime. I learnt a lot doing the prison tours: how to cope with a vocal audiences and hecklers, doing musical numbers and comedy sketches. I enjoyed working with the group and so I signed on for another tour.

Kathy was getting towards the end of her second year at E15 and I had just finished at Stirabout. So we sat down and had a talk about what we were going to do next. I auditioned for a company called Merseyside Young People's Theatre, based in my hometown of Liverpool. This company toured schools and community centres around Merseyside, a theatre-in-education group. I was successful with the audition and they offered me a twelve-month contract which was too good to turn down. Kathy wasn't too happy, and neither was I, that we would be separated for long periods.

E15 used to get Directors to come and watch the 3rd year students at the end of the year in the hope that they would be offered work. Kathy decided to ask if she could audition for one of the Directors even though she was still only at the end of her second year. They agreed and she auditioned for a director called Howard Lloyd Lewis who was the Artistic Director of The Library Theatre in Manchester. He was about to produce a season of musicals at The Wythenshawe Forum which was part of the Library Theatre. As Kathy has a wonderful singing voice he thought she would be an asset to the company and offered her a job with an Equity Card for the forthcoming season. It was too good an opportunity to miss and so she left E15 that summer and started at the Library in September.

So we moved to Liverpool in the summer of 1980.

John McArdle

We found a flat near Sefton Park about five miles from where my mother lived so we could visit often. Kathy's first production was *Piaf*, in which she played Madeleine, Piaf's secretary and chorus. My old mate Seamus started at the Library at the same time as Kathy and they were in many shows together. Things were moving along really well, we were both in work for a long period and we could come home every night, even though my work was in the daytime and Kathy's was day and night.

In those days if you were signed up to do a season in rep, you had to perform your current play in the evenings and rehearse the next play in the day. This was every three to four weeks. They were long days, from 10am to 10.30pm, and all that for £100 a week. My work with Merseyside Young People's Theatre was hard work but very rewarding. We would usually do two shows a day, Monday to Friday, 10 till 5, so it was like a normal day job. It was bringing theatre into the classrooms of children, aged from 5 to 15 depending on the play. This was probably their first experience of theatre so you had to get it right. The director, writers and actors had quite a responsibility, because if you got it wrong, and sometimes we did, it could put them off theatre for life.

I remember doing a historical play to a class of 6 to 8 year-olds in Kirkby. After the show we always asked the kids what they thought of it. On this occasion one little freckle-faced boy told me it was *a pile of shite*, and to be honest he wasn't wrong. You cannot underestimate children; they know more than you think and they speak the truth.

Kathy did her first big pantomime, playing Cinderella. She sang and looked beautiful in the part. I took Justin to see it and this was a turning point in his relationship with Kathy. He was only ten at the time and he really enjoyed the panto and especially seeing Kathy as Cinderella. From then on they became the best of friends.

My contract came to an end before Kathy's; also she had been offered the next season at the Library Theatre. So it made sense that we made our base in Manchester, as she would be there for at least another year. We moved from Liverpool to Chorlton-cum-Hardy in Manchester. We found a nice little bedsit in Hastings Avenue, close to shops and pubs. It was only small but we did it up and made it home. The flat was at the top of the large Victorian building. You came in the door and there was a table and chairs, a settee, and a double bed under the bay window overlooking the street. There was a tiny kitchen off the main room and a tiny bathroom off the kitchen. But we loved it and we were happy in our little nest.

Before Kathy started her next season at the Library Theatre, we decided to take our first holiday together. So off we went to the travel agents and asked them to find us a cheap holiday in the sun. They came up with two weeks in the south of France in a tent for £69. We took it. We travelled to France on a coach with a stopover in Paris at a campsite in the heart of the city – very romantic. We arrived at our destination the next day. It was a huge campsite in a place called Biot, a small village in between Nice and Antibes. It was beautiful, the sun was shining and we were in love. Because we were short of money we would buy food from the local markets and cook dinner at night with a nice bottle of wine. In the day we just lived on bread, cheese and tomatoes. The train service was great and cheap so we travelled to Nice, Monaco and just across the border to Italy. One day we took the train to Monaco to people watch and look at the beautiful architecture. The casino was open in the day, but the gaming tables were closed and only the fruit machines were in use. I decided to do a little gambling and put 10 francs in the slot machines. After my third or fourth go I hit the jackpot, and the machine started pumping out lots and lots of coins. I thought *that's it, we're rich*. When I took it to the cashier to change it, it came to about £60, nearly the cost of our holiday. So to celebrate our winnings we decided to splash out on a meal in a restaurant.

We went to a little restaurant in Juan-les-Pins. It was a beautiful setting, and we sat outside with a view of the ocean, the was food excellent and it seemed like paradise. One day we walked along the promenade in Cannes and thought about how this was where all the film stars came to show off their new films at the festival. I remember saying to Kathy that one day I would come here with a film and I'll tell you more about that later dad. I was so impressed by this part of France; it has a sort of old glamour to it, a very stylish place with a great atmosphere. It makes you feel rich even if you're not; there is so much character in the place. We loved it.

Two weeks later we were back in rainy Manchester. Kathy started back at the Library and I was out of work. Kathy was now doing leads in musicals. One in particular was Brecht's *Happy End* with music by Kurt Weill. Kathy played the lead character Halleluiah Lill. I went to see it on her opening night and I was so proud of her. She was magnificent as Lill; her acting and singing were superb. The whole production was so good I went to see it about five or six times.

I needed to get a job, as it had been four weeks since I was back from my holidays and I was itching to get back to work. Especially after seeing *Happy End*. It made me want to do work like that, of a high standard.

I still had no agent, so it was a matter of writing off to all the reps in the North West with my photo and CV. From that I got an audition with Contact Theatre, a company that was part of the University of Manchester. I was successful and they offered me a season with them. They had a great season to offer me, a devised play to take into the community, called *Flash Gorton* in which I played Flash, *Lulu* in which I played Rodrigo Quast the acrobat (I knew acrobatics would come in handy someday) *Twelfth Night* and a Christmas show. That kept me busy for a while. Richard Williams was the Artistic Director at the time and he asked me if I would like to do another season with them. I didn't hesitate: I said yes. I was learning so much about my craft and getting paid for it. Kathy and I had a great circle of friends on the theatre scene, and some are still our friends today. We would go and see each other's shows and go the wrap parties and meals, it was a great life.

I worked with a director who fulfilled one of my early ambitions. His name was Bob Eaton, a really nice guy and a wonderful director. He was working at Contact Theatre with me, when he was appointed the new Artistic Director of the Liverpool Everyman Theatre. He asked to see me one day. It was to ask me if I would be interested in joining his company in Liverpool. The first play they would be doing was *Lennon*, a musical play about the life of John Lennon, who had just died in New York. It was a fantastic opportunity; I would be working in my home-town again, only this time in one of the best theatres in the country. I couldn't wait to start. Because of Kathy's commitment to her theatre, we decided to stay in Manchester and I would commute. Two other actors from Manchester were in the Liverpool Company so we would share the driving. Chris Monks was one of the actors and the Musical Director and the other actor sharing the driving was Graham Fellows. I recognised him because he had made a hit record called 'Gordon is a Moron' under his recording name Jilted John. He is now famous for his comical character John Shuttleworth.

This play about John Lennon was devised by the company, through research and interviews with people that knew Lennon. We met and interviewed people we would be portraying in the play as we wanted to get it right. The actors playing the Beatles were Mark McGann playing John Lennon, Graham Fellows playing Paul McCartney, Carl Chase playing George Harrison and Jonathan Barlow playing the older Lennon and Ringo. Eithne Hannagan played Auntie Mimi, Mia Siterio played Yoko Ono and Phil Whitchurch and myself played everyone else – 28 characters each. It got a lot of media coverage because it was only two years after John's death and the world premiere was in his hometown. The musical play was a huge success and was transferred to the Sheffield

Crucible and then on to a short run in the West End. My reputation as an actor in the North West was growing; I was never out of work, going from one theatre to another. It was the same for Kathy; she was working non-stop.

Then Kathy became pregnant with our first child so she would soon have to slow down. Her last job before giving birth was a pantomime at Wythenshawe Forum playing Fatima in Ali Baba and the Forty Thieves which was a very appropriate name as she was 6 months pregnant by the time it finished and they had to keep letting out her costume. We couldn't stay in our bedsit, so we applied for a council house in Burnley, Kathy's hometown. We would also be near Kathy's parents Joan and Walter, who could help us out with child minding when the time came. When the time came to tell Walter and Joan that Kathy was pregnant Kathy said that I had to do the talking. It was going to be difficult as we weren't married and Kathy's parents were Catholic and old fashioned about these things. I had been married and had a child already so I don't suppose I seemed a great catch for their youngest daughter. We went round one night for a cup of tea and Kathy kept looking at me as if to say when are you going to tell them. Suddenly in the middle of a normal conversation I just blurted out to Walter: "Kathy's having a baby!"

There was a pregnant pause – excuse the pun – and then Walter said, "You'll have to get a bigger car." That broke the tension and from that moment we had their full support.

Burnley was only 26 miles from Manchester and was commutable to most of the theatres and TV companies. We moved to Rossetti Avenue, Burnley just before our daughter was born. It was a three bedroom semi with a large back garden and the rent was cheap. It was April 21st 1982 and the Falklands war was about to get serious. Kathy was due any time and she was getting bored sitting around the house waiting so we went for a drive over into the Ribble Valley, not far from where we lived.

It was a warm spring day and I was driving over some remote countryside when I spotted something in the middle of the road. I stopped the car and got out to see what it was. As I got closer I noticed it was a snake, curled up and asleep. As I got closer it woke up and slithered off into the grass. I couldn't believe it – the first snake I had ever seen in England. We drove on a little further and had a little picnic, it was a beautiful Spring day. On the way home we were driving towards a low bridge, when all of a sudden a very low flying jet streaked past us, so low we could see the pilot in his cockpit. The noise was so loud it made us jump and we had to pull the car over to the side of the road. We were shaken to say the least. It had been an eventful day and it wasn't over yet. That night Kathy went into labour. Our beautiful daughter Katie was born the next day, April 22nd 1982.

Kathy now stayed at home to look after our new baby and I was back in Liverpool doing another stint at the Everyman Theatre. I would drive nearly every day, as I didn't want to miss anything and wanted to help as much as I could. I asked Kathy if she would make an honest man of me and to my delight she said yes. We had some saving to do as we were just about to move to our first mortgaged house. It was 116 Parkinson Street in an area called Burnley Wood. It was a small two-up two-down terraced house with a small yard at the back. It cost us the grand sum of £8,950. It was a nice little street, with mainly old people living in the area, people who had lived there for most of their lives. They were very good neighbours. When Katie was about a year old Kathy got a job at Oldham Coliseum Theatre. Another actor was working there at the time who also lived in Burnley. His name is Malcolm Hebden, and he's now a household name for playing Norris in *Coronation Street*. He lived at the posh end of Burnley and Parkinson St was at the bottom end, so to speak. When Malcolm found out where we lived he jokingly said he could only visit us after dark so he wouldn't be seen in such a poor area! This was before he was well known. We have been friends ever since and now he will visit us in daylight!

John McArdle

Well the time had come for our wedding and it was on a budget so we had to cut a few corners but Joan and Walter kindly helped us out. My family came down from Liverpool and some of them stayed at our place over night; in fact Kathy cooked them breakfast on our wedding morning. We were married at St Mary's Church, Burnley on the 3rd of September 1983 and Kathy looked so beautiful. I felt a very lucky man.

The man who married us was Canon Deany, a great priest with a sense of humour. As I was waiting at the altar for Kathy to make her entrance, he said, "You can nip out the back if you've got cold feet!" but then the organ started to play the Wedding March and he said, "It's too late – we're under starters orders." So the wedding went ahead without a hitch.

The reception was about eight miles away in a small local village called Rimington. One member of my family got lost and another ran out of petrol but it was a great day and Justin was there too to help us celebrate. Some of our pals from Drama School were also there and I think everyone enjoyed themselves.

Being actors just starting out you never turned down work and in this case our honeymoon had to be put on hold, because on the Monday after the wedding Kathy and Katie went off to Lancaster as Kathy was starting work at the Duke's Playhouse and I went off to Chester to start work at the Chester Gateway Theatre. Kathy was going to find the next three months very hard indeed. She managed to get digs with a lady who was also a registered childminder so she could look after Katie whilst Kathy was at work. This was manageable during the rehearsals for the first play, but once the second play went into rehearsal it would be a nightmare. Also Kathy had two very demanding roles to play. She would be playing Isabella in *Measure for Measure* and Polly Peacham in *The Threepenny Opera* – both leading parts. Kathy would finish *Measure for Measure* at 10.30pm, get home for 11.30, Katie would often wake up in the middle of the night and then Kathy had to get up early to start rehearsals on the next play. She also had to go through the heartbreaking part of leaving Katie with the childminder every morning and not seeing her all day and night. I had it easy; I was doing one play, and once that play was on I had my days free, but Lancaster was too far for me to help out with Katie. I used to pick them up on Saturday night and we would spend Sunday together at home before heading back on Monday morning. It was a challenging time.

The play I was doing at Chester was *Macbeth* and I was playing Banquo. I found it a very exciting experience. It was set in the modern day and was very macho. It had a very good cast: Louis Mellis playing Macbeth and Michelle Newell playing Lady Macbeth, with Ron Donachie as Macduff. Louis Mellis was so dangerous on stage; he was a complete method actor. I had never seen an actor take such risks, sometimes they worked and sometimes not, but he had such courage. When I was not on stage I would watch him from the wings. He would do something different every night, which some of the other actors hated. I didn't mind – it kept you on your toes and made you listen. Louis had such a great imagination; he later went on to write award-winning screenplays such as *Sexy Beast* and *Gangster Number 1*. He also played Stanley Kowalski in *A Streetcar Named Desire* at the Bolton Octagon with Kathy playing Stella and Susanna York playing Blanche DuBois. It was a brilliant production directed by my friend Andy Hay. Kathy was nominated for Best Supporting Actress in the Manchester Evening News Awards for her performance as Stella.

Going back to the Macbeth production. I remember my mother and some of the family coming to see me in it. It was their first time seeing a Shakespeare play and it was great to have their support even though I knew it might not be their cup of tea. They were sitting quite near the front and I could see them out of the corner of my eye. When I made my first appearance as Banquo at the beginning of the play, I heard one of my sisters say quite loudly:

"Look, there's our John!"

Then I could hear the boiled sweets being passed around to the annoyance of the Shakespeare snobs. The best moment was when Macduff's children are being murdered and I heard my Mum say quite loudly, "There's no need for that."

My family were very supportive of me in my early years as an actor and I thank them for that.

So Kathy had finished in Lancaster and I had finished in Chester and it was a bit of relief to have some time off and be together for a while. It was not long before the work came in again and I went off to do my first TV job, a small part in *Coronation Street* playing a character called Scouse Sammy, a truck driving friend of Eddy Yates. It was one day's filming on location, so I didn't get to see the famous *Corrie* set. I did my scenes in a truck talking on the CB radio, so I didn't even get to work with Geoff Hughes.

We had lived in Parkinson Street for just over two years and it was time to move on. In that short time the area was getting a bit rougher, the older people were moving into care homes and our new neighbours were a bit on the noisy side, doing DIY in the middle of the night and pinching clothes off the washing line. We managed to sell with a profit and we moved to a bigger house on the other side of the town. Kathy had been up for a part in a long running drama series for schools called *How We Used to Live*, a very good period drama. She got one of the main characters in the show and it was a long contract, 9 months, which in TV is a long time. This was going to make us more financially secure, so we could afford to pay for childcare and have a holiday.

My next part on the small screen was in a TV film called *Charlie*, directed by Martin Campbell, who later went on to direct some of the Bond films. I played a shop steward of a big union and the scene I had was with the lead actor David Warner. In the scene I had to confront David Warner's character and give him a shove and walk away. So we had a short rehearsal for the crew, then we went for the first take. I did the dialogue with David then I shoved him at the end of the scene, only I shoved him a little too hard, so he went flying over some boxes and landed on his arse.

"Cut, cut, cut!" the director shouted. He took me to one side and said, "I know you're new to film work, John, and you're very good at it, but try not to kill the money."

By 'the money' he meant David Warner, the star of the film. If I'd injured him it would have cost the production company hundreds of thousands of pounds in delays to the filming. So I took it easy after that. That was my method training: I was trying to make the violence real, when really it's all about acting. I was learning more every day. That's one thing they didn't teach you at drama school in those days, film and television technique. Now of course there are plenty of courses that do acting for the camera.

I went back to the Contact Theatre to work with one of my favourite directors, Peter Fieldson. The play was *Accidental Death of an Anarchist* and in the cast were two people that I would become great friends with and still am to this day; Andy Hay and Sue Johnston. We had such fun working together on this play. It's one of those moments in your career that you realise how lucky you are to be part of this family. I know that sounds very corny, but it was a real appreciation of what you are part of. A new television channel had just been created and one of their first programmes to be commissioned was a new soap created by Phil Redmond, called *Brookside*. We were in the dressing room one night and Sue said her agent got her an audition for this new programme. She went along the next day and the following week they had offered her the iconic part of Shelia Grant. She was over the moon, a year's contract on TV it was wonderful for her.

Kathy had been working on *How We Used to Live* now for the past six months. She was enjoying it and had made some good friends. I would go along to meet Kathy at work sometimes, so I got to know her fellow actors and directors. On one of these occasions I got talking to Carol Wilkes, a director and producer on the show and she asked me what I was up to. At the time I was not working, so she asked me if I would like to do an episode of the programme. Of course I would! When I got the script I noticed my scenes were with Maggie, Kathy's character and I was to play a doctor who would come to visit her sick young son. Maggie was a very working class mill worker with a young family and I was her local GP.

In the scene I had with Kathy I had to examine her son then have a private word with her about what was wrong with him. This was the first time we had worked together professionally and it was very strange. When I delivered my first line to Kathy, she just cracked up and couldn't keep a straight face. My hair was parted in the middle, I had on this baggy suit and was talking in a posh accent. In the end neither of us could do the scene for laughing. It took about eight takes to get it right. Carol said afterwards that was the last time she would cast us opposite each other. It was a long time before we did work together, but it was a joy working with Kathy. She is such a good actress with a great sense of humour and a great team player.

Not long after that I got my second crack at *Coronation Street*. This time it was two episodes and all my scenes were in the Rover's Return. I was a little more nervous this time as I would be meeting and working with people that I had grown up watching since I was a little kid.

I walked into the Green Room after I had been into makeup and wardrobe and was standing around like a lost soul, when Jean Alexander, who played Hilda Ogden came up to me and said in a posh voice:

"Is no one looking after you love?"
I was lost for words. "*Er I don't think so,*" I eventually replied.

She then got out a schedule and put me right and told one of the runners to look after me. What a lovely lady. She taught me something that day about looking after new people who join an established cast. It can be a difficult and daunting experience and I'm always mindful to help put people at their ease. After all we've all been the new guy at some point. Just before I was about to start filming I went into the gents – it was nerves. I was standing in the cubicle having a pee, when Christopher Quinten, the actor who played Brian Tildsley came and stood next to me.

He was wearing a pair of short shorts and a vest, looking very tanned and asked. "How long are you in the street for?"
"Just the two episodes," I replied.

He went on to tell me that you had to do at least six months to get the hang of it. Having said that he zipped up and left. I went to the sink to wash my hands. One of the cubicle doors opened and out came Bryan Mosley, who played Alf Roberts. He joined me at the sink.
Having heard my conversation with Chris Quinten he said: "Take no notice of him, he's been here 10 years and he still hasn't got the hang of it."
He then took me to the set and put me in the safe hands of the first assistant director. I was working mainly with Julie Goodyear, who played Bet Lynch. I found her to be friendly, charming and with a wicked sense of humour. She was a joy to work with and my experience working on *Corrie* was a good one.

The Small Screen

Television work started to come in a lot more now; my name was slowly becoming familiar with the casting directors. The agent I had at the time was not very good; she mainly represented extras and variety artists. A group of actors that lived in Hebden Bridge, West Yorkshire, were forming an actor's cooperative and asked me if I wanted to join them. I did and we formed a company called 'North of Watford'. There were twelve actors in all, six men and six women. We would represent each other for all types of acting work: TV, film, theatre, radio, commercials, voiceovers, anything really that would cover professional acting. We would arrange the interviews and negotiate the fees. You had to man the office when you were not working, on a rota basis. I found this difficult at first, as I was not trained as an agent, but in time learned to cope with it. I was offered the part of a teacher in the programme Sue Johnston had joined a year previously, Brookside. I was so excited to be working with Sue again and to be part of this new soap that was proving very popular, especially among young people.

Brookside was an independent TV series run by its creator Phil Redmond for Channel 4. It was still very much in its infancy and there were a lot of teething problems to start with. It was unique in that it was set on a real housing estate in a suburb of Liverpool. There was no studio at all. Everything was done on site. Phil Redmond had bought all the houses connected with the characters in the show and other houses for production. So it was written, shot and edited all on Brookside Close.

I arrived on my first day of filming at the security gate at the end of the close. The security guard directed me to the wardrobe department to get into costume. There didn't seem to be anyone around to ask what I should be wearing. One of the canteen ladies helped me in the end: she found a suit with a note pinned to it. On the note it said, *To the actor playing Mr Todd*, (that was me) *hope it fits, see you on the set.* So I got into the suit (luckily it did fit) and then I had to find out what I did next. There still didn't seem to be anyone about so I sat in the canteen waiting for someone to come and get me.

After about two hours a young runner came up to me and said: "Are you the bloke playing Mr Todd?"

I replied that I was.

"Sorry we're running late, mate, come with me and I'll get you to the set."

We arrived at the set, a school classroom in a disused school about a mile away. The director Chris Clough introduced himself and then went on say he had changed the dialogue in the first scene I was doing and could I just learn it in ten minutes. This was a bit much, I had learned a long speech to the class of extras playing the school children and I had to forget that and learn this new one in a matter of minutes. Well after about ten takes we got it in the can. My next scene was with one of the regular characters. So the floor manager asked one of his assistants where she was.

"Don't know," came the reply.

"Well where the fuck is she?" asked the director.

We couldn't do the scene without her so there was a search on. They sent runners into Liverpool city centre to look for her, as she liked to go shopping when not working. So we were all sitting around doing nothing for two hours until they finally found her in some café in the middle of town. Someone on the crew had released her early, which is why she was missing so it wasn't really her fault. It was about 7pm when we finished.

You had to admire Phil Redmond for what he brought to British television and Liverpool with the creation of Brookside. This new soap he'd created was the first time since *Coronation Street* that a gritty episodic drama had hit the mass audience. It reflected day-to-day issues of ordinary people and it did so with humour and great writing. Phil also employed local people to work on the programme, creating lots of apprenticeships in the technical crew. Also the characters on the show reflected a cross section of society. It was Channel 4's flagship and it was great to be a small part of it. I was asked back on a number of occasions to play Mr Todd or 'Sweeney Todd' as the pupils named him.

While I was doing a Christmas show at the Chester Gateway theatre, my agency called and said that Brookside had been on and would I go in the following Sunday to do another episode. The scene I had to do was with Sue's character, Sheila Grant and her husband Bobby, played by Ricky Tomlinson. It was quite a long scene for television, about 6 pages, so I had to learn it very quickly, as well as doing 3 shows a day at Chester. The night before the *Brookie* job I had been to a party after work and drank a little too much. The next day, the filming day, I was hungover so badly I could hardly get out of bed. In this business there's no such thing as throwing a sickie, you go in even if you've just had major surgery. When I went into makeup I looked like a ghost, so they had to patch me up so I didn't frighten the viewers.

Sue said, "Oh dear, let's get this scene done then poor John can go home to bed."

This scene was going to take at least two hours, because it was on single camera and it had to be shot from every angle. The director knew nothing of my hangover, but he was about to. I was in the middle of this epic scene when I started to feel like I was about to throw up. So when the director shouted cut, I got up and rushed to the bathroom to be sick. I would come back and start the scene again, after makeup had powdered me down to take the perspiration of my face. Every time we cut I would bolt for the toilet. In the end the director realised what was going on and told me that even in the middle of a take, just to go if I felt sick. That was very understanding of him but I got through it.

I continued to work at the Everyman Theatre in Liverpool. It was one of my favourite theatres. The next play I was to do there was a new musical drama written by Bob Carlton and directed by Bob and *Brookside* director Chris Clough. It was about the ghost of Bill Shankley, the famous Liverpool football club manager. The title part was to be played by a famous Scottish comedian called Chic Murray. I had never seen Chic's act before and neither had most of the cast as we were too young, so we didn't know his genius as a comic. At the read through you could hardly hear him, he just mumbled, so you didn't know if he had finished his line or not. It was really hard work but Chic was an eccentric and his humour was an acquired taste.

On the opening night of the play Chic just walked on and got a standing ovation. All his fans had turned up. All he had to do was stand there and they laughed. I was playing second lead so most of my scenes were with Chic, and that was a test of my tolerance. Comedians of his generation find it hard to stick to a script and to share the stage. It's not their fault, they feel the need to steal every scene and they do it well, but at the expense of the other actors.

On one particular night, Chic had forgotten his lines, and there was this long pause, so I waited and was about to cover up, when Chic turned to the audience and said, pointing at me, "He's forgotten his lines!"

This got a huge laugh and as we were going off into the wings, Chic turned to me and said "Shall we keep that in?"

John McArdle

I and some other members of the cast didn't think it was a good play at all but the audiences did and it got extended. Bob and Chris knew I was having a tough time with Chic and appreciated my patience with him. They said they would repay me one day and sure enough they did. The title of that play was *You'll Never Walk Alone*, but the cast called it 'You'll Never Work Again'. In the last week of the show Bob Carlton had a word with me. He was about to make his debut as a TV director on *Brookside*. He told me that they were bringing in a new family to the Close and that I fitted the bill as the head of that family. I told him I'd already had a recurring character in the programme and that would rule me out. It was six or seven months since I had been in the show, so he told me to get on to my agent and he would even put a word in for me with Chris Clough who was already a director at *Brookside*. The next thing my agency rang to tell me that I had an interview at *Brookside* for the new family.

I didn't think I had much of a chance, having done about seven episodes as Mr Todd, but what the hell, I had nothing to lose. I decided to go in as this character they were looking for. The description for Billy Corkhill was Liverpool male, 33, working class man, electrician, buying his first house with his wife and two children, a boy, 13 and a girl, 14. I was originally cast as a teacher in *Brookside* because in their eyes I was lower middle class; I didn't have a strong Liverpool accent naturally because I had spent so much time away from my city of birth. So I went into the interview wearing a leather jacket and jeans and talking in my strongest Scouse accent. I was interviewed by Phil Redmond, the creator of the programme and Dorothy Andrews, the casting director. The first part of the meeting was to talk about myself, was I married etc and then we read some of the script they had written for the new family. We then went on to do some improvisations. I was there for about 2 hours, longer than normal auditions. I went home feeling exhausted, but I had done my very best. The next day my agency rang and told me that they liked me and that I had a call back for the next day.

On the call back day I did improvisations with different actresses auditioning for the part of Billy's wife Doreen. I was there for most of the day, working with about six or seven different actresses. The next day they asked me if I would come back and work with the actors that were auditioning for the children. It was now nearing the end of the week and they still hadn't let me know if I was in with a chance or not. I didn't know how many other blokes were up for this part. It was now Thursday and we had started these interviews on the Monday so I was hoping they would let me know soon. They called me in on the Friday to discuss what I thought of a certain actress who had auditioned with me, and which kids I thought were suitable. They thanked me and said they would let me know. But when would they let me know? It was like torture, doing all this work and then not knowing what their decision would be. I got home at about 3pm that day and told Kathy that I couldn't have done any more to get that part.

At 5pm the phone rang. I was a little scared to pick up the phone – was it then and was it going to be bad news? Kathy stood next to me by the phone waiting to see what my reaction would be. My agent said that Mersey Television would like to offer me the part of Billy Corkhill in *Brookside*, a 12 month contract or 52 guaranteed episodes. I was trying to keep calm, but this was fantastic: a year's work in prime time TV. Yes, yes, of course I would do it that's what I had been busting my gut for all week. I put the phone down, we were so excited! This was it, we could have a holiday and a decent car, and most of all financial security for the next year. This was my big break. I had been out of drama school for five years, working constantly in rep and small parts in TV and now at the grand old age of 35 I had got where I wanted to be, doing a job that I absolutely loved and getting well paid for it. Our lives were about to change for the better.

John McArdle

Me as a young Para

Me on the roof of our flat in Bondi 1970

You Never Said Goodbye

Standing by my Mini, Fremantle 1972

My 22nd birthday on Bougainville Island, with two friends

123

John McArdle

Myself and a friend scaffolding in the north west cape of Australia

Kathy E15 in 1981

Photo still from Brookside. Alan Igbon on my right

Original To poster with Sue Johnston

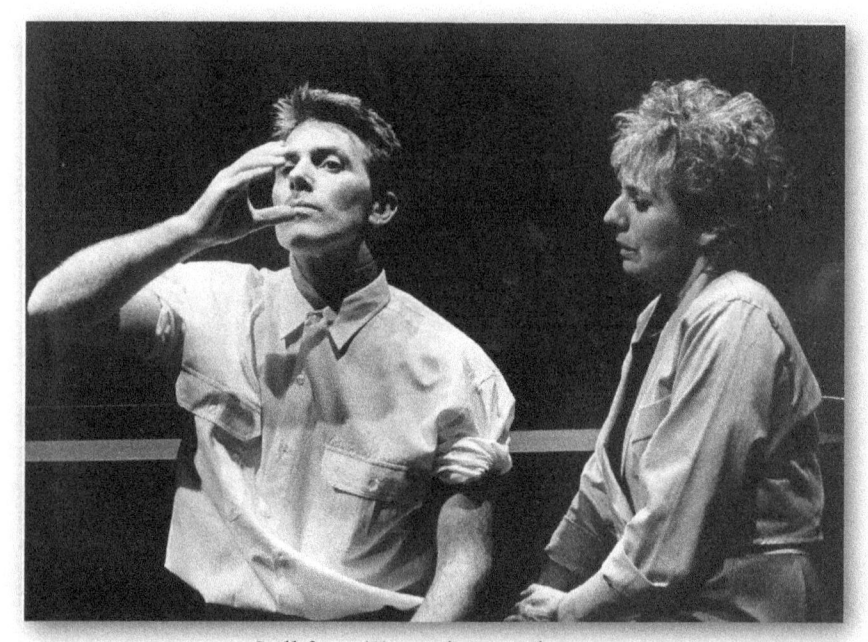

John McArdle

Still from To, with Sue Johnston

Inmates of Underbelly. With our producer Eileen Quinn far left.

Brookside

The other actors making up the Corkhill family were Kate Fitzgerald playing Doreen, Jason Hope, playing Rod and Justine Kerrigan playing Tracy. Our first episode was us moving in to Number 10 Brookside Close. As we moved in, a funeral was in progress for one of the unfortunate casualties of soap stardom, written out and never to return. We were a bit stiff in the beginning of our debut as the Corkhills, but soon got into the rhythm of things and fitted in like a glove. At the beginning of our work on *Brookie*, Phil Redmond told us to go and watch some of the filming we were not involved in and see how the system worked, to get a feel for the style and mood of the programme. Two well-established actors in the show at the time were about to do a scene and we were invited to go and watch. The actors in question where Betty Alburge, playing Edna Cross and Bill Dean, playing Harry Cross. These were the senior characters in the Close. The scene they had to do was a simple one. Harry and Edna were in their front room. Edna had to approach the window and watch a car drive out of the close and her line was, 'They've gone' then Harry had a long speech to say.

Bill was well known for getting his scene done on the first take, but if they had to go again he had trouble remembering his lines. The director said, *action*, and Betty approached the window.

"They're here." she said.
"Cut!" said the director. "The line is 'they've *gone*'. Ok, let's go again."

So Betty approached the window again and this time she said, "Where are they?"

"That's not the line, Betty, let's go again."

By this time poor Bill was having a panic attack, thinking if she doesn't get this right soon he will never remember his long speech. So they do another five or six takes but poor Betty was having a bad senior moment. The director was very patient and didn't lose his rag at all. He took Betty to one side and repeated her line to her: *They've gone, they've gone, they've gone!* He gestured to the cameraman to roll tape, then told Betty to go to the window and say the line.

Betty reached the window and said the immortal line, "They've gone." Then Bill said, "So have I.'

Poor Bill, after all that time he'd dried on *his* speech. It was going to be a long day!

Don't get me wrong, actors have good days and bad days, but as you get older learning lines at such a rate as they do in soaps is bloody hard work. It was hard work if you were in a major storyline and the Corkhills were at the beginning because we had to establish ourselves as new characters and the public had to get to know us. The general public didn't like us at first. This was normal. The soap had been going for two years and the fans had invested their time and emotions in the programme and deserved to have their say, so it took a little time for them to accept you. And they did after we had been on screen for about three months.

I used to commute from Burnley every day, but if it was a heavy week I would stop at my mother's, who only lived two miles from *Brookside*. I had been on air for about four weeks and people in the street were beginning to recognise me. It was quite nice, they would ask for your autograph and shout your character name out in the street, and they talked to you as if you were really the character you played on screen. I remember one time I was off for the weekend and was relaxing at home with the family on a Saturday afternoon and a knock came on the door so I went to answer it. I opened the door to a man similar age to myself.

"So you do live here!"
"Yes, afraid so," I replied.
He complimented me on my performance in *Brookie* and told me how much he liked the show, and then he said, "Right can you come down to my house and wish my daughter a happy birthday?"
"Where do you live?"
"Just about half a mile away, that's all."

I told him it was a bit inconvenient, as it was my day off and I was spending some precious time with my own family. He then went into a rant about what a stuck up actor I was and that I had no time for my fans. That was the down side to being in the public eye, but on the whole people were nice to me and I didn't mind signing autographs. In fact I was flattered that people asked me and I felt lucky to be in this position.

After a year in *Brookside* things had changed so much for me and my family. We were secure financially and had started to be able to take lovely holidays in Florida. We went to Disney Land and Clearwater Beach. We had come a long way from sleeping in a tent for two weeks, although I must say that camping holiday in the South of France was one of the best we ever had. When they offered me another year's contract, we decided to move house again. This time we moved to the outskirts of Burnley to a small village called Cliviger. The house was semi-detached with a small garden but one of the most breathtaking views of the countryside. It was to be our home for the next thirteen years.

By now the Corkhills were well established on the Close and well liked. Working on *Brookside* was a joy; the cast and crew were just one big happy family. We worked hard doing two half hour episodes a week, but we also had fun doing it. It was great to be working with Sue Johnston again. We became great friends and Kathy and I still socialise with her and her family to this day. There were some wonderful actors on the show, people like Ricky Tomlinson, Paul Usher, Kate Fitzgerald, Mickey Starke and many more. The crew were second to none; they were great to work with. One guy in particular, who sadly is no longer with us, was Graham Edgerton, or Chewy as we called him, he was an electrician or a 'spark'. He was such a great guy. He would even tell you truthfully what he thought of your performance, and he was usually right. If he thought you were crap in a scene, I would ask the director if I could go again.

So many people who were trained in film and TV at *Brookie* went on to become very successful in their future careers. One of the country's most successful writers, Jimmy McGovern started on *Brookie*. Terry McDonough started as a trainee cameraman and is now a respected director working in America on such programmes as *Breaking Bad*. Ken Horn who started off as a cameraman and director went on to produce such shows as *Heartbeat* and *The Royal*. This was the same for actors such as Anna Friel, Sue Johnston, Ricky Tomlinson, Amanda Burton and Michael Starke. One great success story that came out of the programme was Mal Young; he started on *Brookside* in the props department, when I first started in 1985. He then became a floor manager, then production manager, moving on to assistant producer and by the time I left in 1990 he was Producer. In the space of 5 years Mal had worked his way to the top job. That was the sort of opportunity Phil Redmond gave to people that worked hard and had the talent. After leaving *Brookside* Mal went on to great things, eventually becoming Head of Drama at the BBC, then onto producing in America.

Brookside was watched by about 8 million people at one time and reached a wide audience young and old. It reflected what was happening in everyday life, not just in Liverpool, but the whole nation. My second year in *Brookside* was much easier, because I was now established and started to get some good story lines. At the time the country was going through economic hardship and Billy Corkhill was an ordinary man trying to cope with unemployment and looking after his family the best he could. In fact he was one of the working class victims of Thatcher's Britain. So Billy had to do anything to get money to pay his mortgage and bills and cope with his wife's spending habits. He got involved in insurance scams, working on the side, and even armed robbery – which all meant good drama. When we were doing the armed robbery storyline, we were joined by a wonderful actor by the name of Alan Igbon; he was playing the ringleader of the armed robbery gang. We had just finished a day's filming together and were walking to the car park. At the entrance to the car park, which was at the far end of the Close, the autograph hunters usually gathered to pounce on you as you left for home.

This little 8 year-old scally kid, (this is a streetwise Liverpool lad) came running up to me and said, "Billy give us your autograph, mate!"

So I did, then asked him, "Don't you want Alan's?"

The kid looked at Alan scornfully. "Why would I want his autograph, he's not even in Brookside."

Little did this kid know but Alan had starred in the much acclaimed *Boys from the Black Stuff* and many more wonderful TV dramas.

"He will be in it soon. We're just filming his stuff at the moment, so he'll be on screen in a few weeks."

The kid gave him a look him up and down and spoke to me as if Alan didn't exist at that moment: "Ok, when he's been on Brookie, I'll ask him then. See ya, Billy!" and off he went.

A few weeks later, after Alan's episodes had gone out he told me that the kid asked for his autograph the previous night. He said he was walking to the car park and the same kid we'd met a few weeks before approached him and asked for his autograph. So he obliged and wrote his signature on the lad's piece of paper. The kid looked at what Alan had written and asked him what it said.

"It's my name, Alan Igbon."
The kid scrunched up the autograph and said: "Don't put that, put Billy's mate."

We used to get some really good actors joining the show for short periods, because the show had a great reputation in the business.

One thing the company should have done was give advice on how to handle press interviews, especially the tabloids. If you have never given interviews before you tend to be too honest and give the press a little too much information that could be misinterpreted. I gave my first big page interview to one of the Sunday tabloids. I wanted to talk about me as an actor and my part in *Brookside* and a little about my family and hobbies. At the time Kathy had done a TV drama opposite Dennis Waterman, it was called *Who's Our Little Jenny Lind* and Kathy had some love scenes with Dennis in the drama. The programme was to be screened on the Sunday that my article came out. The reporter asked me what I thought of Dennis and my wife doing love scenes. I told him that we were both actors and from time to time we both had to do such scenes, it was part of our job.

He then went on to ask me:
"Aren't you a little jealous of another man kissing your wife in front of the whole nation?" "Well, I am only human," I said, "Of course it's not very nice to watch that sort of thing, even though there is nothing in it."

I came to regret saying this. They took a few photos and said that the article will be mainly about me and *Brookside*. A few weeks later the article came out, so off I went to the newsagents to get a copy. Kathy and I sat down at the kitchen table with a cup of coffee to read the article together. It was a double page spread in the middle of the paper and its headline was

JOHN HATES WIFE'S LOVE SCENES WITH DENNIS WATERMAN. We looked at each other, stunned. Kathy was shocked and embarrassed and rightly so. I explained to Kathy that I had only mentioned at the end of a long interview that it was normal for a man to be a little jealous under those circumstances. But it was too late they had turned my interview in to something I never said and made me look a fool.

My mother rang me up a few seconds later saying what a good article it was, and that it shows you how much you love your wife. My mother always sees the positive side of things. After that I was more careful in doing interviews with the press. They are not all bad but you have to be on your guard. I did meet up with Dennis Waterman later and apologised for what they had written. He was great about it and told me not to worry it happened to him all the time. It was all part of a learning curve in dealing with being in the public eye.

Sometimes you tend to forget that people know who you are. Just because they don't come up and ask for your autograph doesn't mean that they don't recognise you. I was staying over at my mother's house one night, as she lives near the *Brookside* set. I decided to get a taxi to work the next day instead of using the car. You didn't need to phone a taxi as they used to park up at the pub across the road from my mum's house. So I jumped into the nearest cab and told the driver to take me to Brookside. On the journey he was unusually quiet for a Liverpool cab driver and didn't have much to say. I was the one trying to make conversation. When we reached the gates of the set I asked him how much.

He said, "There's no charge."

"Come on," I replied, "You've got a living to make, I don't want a freebie."

"I am not a taxi," he said. "I was just parked in the car park waiting for my girlfriend and you jumped into the back of my car and said 'Take me to Brookside', so I have."

I couldn't believe it. This guy had stood his girlfriend up to bring me to work for nothing. I asked him why he did it.

He said, "Well if Billy Corkhill jumps in the back of your car and tells you to take him to work, you do."

I told him to wait a moment and I would be back with a note for his girlfriend. I went into publicity and got a set of the cast-signed photos and signed my own personally to his girlfriend with a note saying why he was late. He was made up with that and drove off. People on the whole are nice especially when they can empathise with a particular character and a lot of people did feel sympathy for Billy's situation.

One thing that being in soap does for an actor is to give you a sense of security in this somewhat precarious job. To have your contract renewed on an annual basis and to be able to plan ahead is one of the main reasons people stay in soaps for such a long time. And who can blame them? You're doing a job you absolutely love, being well paid and receiving recognition for it, what more could you ask for in life?

But I had become an actor to play different roles and work with a wide variety of people. I had been playing the same character for nearly five years now and I was almost forty. I had to fit a lot more in if I wanted a varied career. So I had a discussion with Kathy about leaving *Brookside* when my contract came to an end and she was totally behind me in what I wanted to do. It meant I had some decision making to do in the not too distant future. The storylines at the time where about Billy and Sheila getting together, so I was working with my good friend Sue Johnston. At that time Andy Hay was artistic director of the Bolton Octagon Theatre and the Writer in Residence was Jim Cartwright, one of our country's greatest playwrights. Andy knew Sue and I were itching to do some theatre again, but were restricted at the time because Phil Redmond's policy was that none of his actors could do any outside work while under contract. Meanwhile Andy had approached Jim Cartwright to write a two-hander for Sue and myself. Jim was a fan and relished the project but we didn't know if we would we get permission from Phil. Sue, Andy and I had a meeting with Phil to try and persuade him to release us for a couple of months to do this play. Phil agreed on the basis that the play would be the only thing we would be permitted to do outside of our Brookside commitment. So Jim, Andy, Sue and I had a meeting to discuss what the play could be about and Jim then would go away and write it in his unique style. We all chipped in ideas about where it was set, what type of characters were in it, anything as far away as possible from the characters we portrayed in Brookside. I had just seen a film called *Barfly* with Mickey Rourke and Faye Dunaway, about a couple of drunks that form their relationship in different bars across the city, so I suggested that maybe it should be set in a pub where there was potential for all sorts of interesting characters. After the meeting Jim went off to write and said he would call us in for a reading when he was nearer to finishing the play.

After about three months, Andy and Jim called Sue and I in for a reading of the first draft of the play he had written, which had no title as yet. It was set in a Northern pub and consisted of about 28 characters involved in pub life, to be played by just Sue and myself. The reading was a little hard to cope with sometimes, as I would be talking to myself as two different characters. But we knew straight away that this was the start of a very fine play. Jim realised that some of the scenes he had written would be impossible to do and went away to write another draft, taking our limitations into consideration. He came back three weeks later with another draft. This time the characters had been culled down to about seven each which was much more doable, and he had kept the best characters from his first draft. He also had a title, and was calling the play 'To'. We asked him why this title and he told us he had wanted to write a play with the shortest title. His last play was 'Bed' and before that 'Road'. Also "To" was a play on the word two, as in two people (He later retitled the play 'Two'). From there we went into rehearsals for 'To' for the next three and a half weeks.

John McArdle

It was great to be working with the writer as we could discuss things with him and then he would go home and do some re-writes for the next day. Doing a two hander means there is quite a lot to remember, especially from two actors that have been away from the stage for such a long period: eight years in Sue's case and five years for myself. The play was full of interesting characters who frequented the pub, run by the Landlord and Landlady, who were the mainstays of the story. Sue played an old lady that cared for her dying husband, a woman who was the other woman in a secret relationship. I played an old man that had lost his wife after many years of a good marriage, and a little boy whose drunken father had left him outside a pub. As a couple we played Fred and Alice, a middle aged couple that had special needs, Moth and Maudie a couple where Moth was a bit of a philanderer. Then we had Mr & Mrs Eiger a huge woman and a weedy man where Sue's character liked big men, and Roy and Lesley whose story was about domestic violence. All in all, there were fourteen characters between us which was a wonderful opportunity for two actors. The opening night was drawing near and Sue and I were getting more and more scared, not just because we had not been on stage for many years but we were to be judged by the TV audience that we had built up over the years. Also the national press would have their pencils sharpened to write their reviews on our performances and on Jim's latest play. So it was very daunting to say the least. Kathy was supportive as ever, saying I would be fine and that had I started out as a stage actor and that you never lose it. I hoped I hadn't. The director Andy Hay had done a brilliant job, Jim had written a piece of pure dramatic poetry, the crew had worked so hard: lighting, set design, costume, props, all had produced a perfect setting for this play, and you didn't want to let them down. Most importantly we didn't want to let ourselves down.

The opening night came and Sue and I had our beginners call. We were standing in the entrance to the stage waiting for the green light. We were debating whether or not to go through with it. *Why did we agree to this madness?* But it was too late: our queue light turned green. We walked out to our theatre in the round to an enormous applause. The full house was a mixture of press, agents, fellow actors, friends and our devoted public. This was a new play, and it had not been tried and tested yet; we were about to find out the verdict in about one hour and twenty minutes. We took our final bow to a standing ovation. It was an unbelievable first night, and they loved it! This is why we do it, for that immediate response to something that has been experienced live. Everyone had loved what they had seen and we were over the moon with how it went. All we had to do now was repeat that performance every night for the next three weeks. Throughout the run we had a mixture of a TV audience and a more traditional theatre going audience. It was the first time some of the audience had been to a theatre play, and this was due to our exposure on prime time television. It felt great to be responsible for that.

One performance was attended by 90% of ladies of a certain age, and in fact when I walked onstage all I could see was a sea of blue rinse. When I came on as the old man that had lost his wife, I had to order a pint at the bar and take a seat at a table very close to the audience. Jim told me that when playing the old man, I had to be brave and leave long pauses in the monologue. So I would say a line then come in after a long pause with the next and so on until I reached the end. Well this old dear sitting very close to me started to try and have a conversation with me.

She first of all said, "Alright, Billy? You look better in the flesh than you do on telly."

This had the audience in stitches, but I had to hold on and try not to laugh.

When I started one of my long pauses, she then jumped in with, "Have you forgotten your lines, Billy?"

The audience were on the floor, and this woman was stealing the show. I managed to get through to the end and as I was walking off she waved and shouted, "You were very good, I'll be coming again".

She didn't come again; if she did, I might have been ready for her. The time seemed to go so fast, and it was coming to an end; we had played to full houses for every performance and it was so refreshing to be in something so successful.

So it was back to *Brookside* to carry on with our day job. This theatre experience had got us thinking: was it time to move on? Sue and I discussed what we were going to when the next contract was to be signed. We both came to the conclusion that we would leave the show at the same time and hopefully do 'To' again. That was the plan: we were to leave *Brookside* in the June, do 'To' in Bolton for a month, then take it to the Edinburgh Fringe in August, then onto the Young Vic in London for three months. This was hopefully going to be our showcase to the casting directors and TV and theatre directors to show we had more to offer than the characters we had been playing for the past eight years. So we left *Brookside* in the summer of 1990. It was sad to leave after five years in one job; I would miss the cast and crew of this wonderful show. I have a lot to thank *Brookside* for; it taught me so much about working in front of a camera and that the technical side of acting in front of a camera is just as important as the performance – in fact it improves the performance. You learn things like hitting marks without looking for them, how big or small your performance should be, depending on the size of the shot, how to relax and get the best out of your scene. After five years of apprenticeship in single camera television, I would be prepared for anything the industry had to offer me.

We had three opening nights to endure again for 'To' - in Bolton, at the Edinburgh fringe, and the Young Vic. You may think it's easy once you've done the play before and that you'd have no worries, but opening nights are stressful no matter how many times you've done it before. You have the national press in and lots of industry people so there's quite a lot riding on it. Even though we had done this play 30 or 40 times it was nerve racking to open again, but the first night of the Bolton Octagon went really well.

You Never Said Goodbye

Just before I left *Brookside* to do *'To'* again I received a fan letter that was to turn into something quite weird. During my period at *Brookside* I received hundreds of fan letters from all types of people young and old, most just asking for a signed photo or an autograph. I even got some letters offering me a job, when my character Billy was unemployed. Most of the mail was from friendly harmless fans, but one particular letter caused me a bit of concern. It started off just saying that she admired Billy Corkhill and could I send her a photo, which I did, as I always answered my fan mail personally. A few weeks later I received a gift from this woman, a knitted scarf and a long letter. The letter was in the form of a poem, but I recognised the words from a Beatle song 'I Want to Hold Your Hand' I didn't reply to this letter and forgot about it until a few weeks later when I received another one. This time the gift was a ring and another long letter saying that she wanted to meet Billy Corkhill and keep him for herself. I found this a little worrying and handed the letters and gifts over to our publicity department. I thought that would be the end of it. But when we started rehearsing the play at Bolton I got another letter from this unknown woman including a copy of the Dali Lama's *Third Eye*. I ignored this letter, and then a week later I received another one. She was angry that I had not replied to her letters. I told Kathy about it and Jim Cartwright and Anne Hornsby the theatre publicity officer.

After the play had been running for about 3 weeks I got a letter from the mysterious woman saying that she was coming to the play and she would meet me after the performance. She did not say what day she was coming and signed off *The Lady in Red*. I was on pins wondering when she would turn up. It got to the last night and I thought that was it - *she's not coming, thank goodness*. As I went out on stage I took a sneaky look at the audience to see who was in and there she was, three rows from the front all in red and wearing dark sunglasses. I had to really concentrate hard to do the show that night, thinking *is this woman going to jump on stage and stab me?!* After the show I got changed and went out front to meet Kathy and the rest of the company. As this was our last night there was a party. There were still quite a few of the punters in the foyer waiting for autographs. Then I finally met the Lady in Red.

At the time I was signing some autographs for a couple of young girls, and she came up to them and told them to keep away from me as I belonged to her. She then turned to me and asked me why I had not replied to her letters and where was the book she'd sent me. She also asked me why I didn't sound like Billy Corkhill and what was I doing playing someone else on this stage? I tried to explain to her that I was not Billy Corkhill, that I was John McArdle, but she didn't want to know. She then gave me a crystal in the shape of a pyramid and told me to think of her when I held it. Kathy must have noticed that I was in trouble and came to my rescue. The lady in red asked who she was and I introduced Kathy as my wife. She wouldn't believe me; she said I was hers alone. Then Jim Cartwright came to the rescue. He took her to one side and explained to her that I was not really Billy Corkhill and that I was happily married to Kathy. In fact Jim was really helpful, he managed to convince this poor woman that I was not who she thought I was and that she would be better off without me. After that night I have thankfully never heard another word from her.

So now we moved up to Edinburgh to do the last two weeks of the Fringe. We were performing at the Pleasance Theatre which was very different from the Octagon. The Octagon was a theatre in the round and the Pleasance was a traditional proscenium arch theatre, so the staging would be completely different. We had no props in the play, as everything was mimed, and when we performed in the round I had it locked in my mind where everything was. Now I had to change all that and it was not an easy thing to do with only a few hours before we opened. When I got back to the digs, I told Jim Cartwright how insecure I felt about the changes and that I was nervous about it. At the time Jim was into hypnosis and offered to practise on me to make me feel more relaxed. After his hypnosis session I felt even worse; my head was all over the place. I expressed my worries to Kathy and Sue and they tried to reassure me that all would be fine and once I got on stage all anxieties would disappear. The national press were in again plus my agent and his friends and a packed house.

The thing about this job is that no matter how bad you feel, physically or mentally, you can't have the day off; you have to go out on that stage. That's what I did; I stepped out into this unfamiliar staging and felt lost. The first scene starts with the landlord and landlady serving imaginary customers and miming getting glasses and bottles from various places in the bar along with some very quick fire dialogue. I bent down to get something from a place I usually go to and to my horror it was wrong, and I couldn't get this out of my mind. Sue gave me a line and I just answered her with the same line I had given her before. She could see the fear in my eyes and looked at me as if to say, *I can't help you*. We managed to get back to the script, but in the next scene I was to walk to the front of the stage and deliver a monologue to the audience. Sue walked off and I walk to the front of the stage. Everything was in slow motion. I could see the audiences smiling faces, anticipating something good coming up. In my head in the few seconds before I was about to do my monologue I didn't have a clue what I was going to say. I wanted to stop and tell the audience that I couldn't go on and that they should ask for their money back. I got to the front of the stage and opened my mouth and the monologue came out, word for word from the script. I came off wondering to myself *how did that happen?* But it wasn't over yet; I was straight back on to do the next scene and so on and so on until the end. I got through the rest of the show without any big mistakes but it was pure hell. I felt so bad for letting this happen, especially on the press night. *What would people think?* I thought I'd been crap. The very opposite happened though. Everyone loved the play and our performances, and no one noticed my mess up in the opening scene – only Sue, Jim, Andy, the crew and Kathy of course. The reviews the next day in the Sunday broadsheets where absolutely wonderful. The next night was going to be hard because I had to exorcise my demons, but I did and the rest of the run went brilliantly.

It was then on to London and the Young Vic and back to performing the play in the round. My sense of security came back straight away. The press night at the Young Vic went without incident – or so I thought. After the play my brothers Rory and Terry told me about some bloke who was sitting next to them who kept writing in a notebook all the time while I was performing on stage. In the interval they approached this gentleman and said if he carried on writing in the second half he would find it difficult to pick up a pen in the future. My lovely brothers were trying to protect me from this ignorant oaf who was writing during the performance. The man in question said he was doing his job and that he had to take notes during a performance.

"What kind of job is that?" enquired Rory.

The man explained that he was a theatre critic and he was writing a review on the play.

Terry then said, "You better give him a good one then. Enjoy the show".

I love them for this. They never go to the theatre and here they were supporting me and in their way protecting me, especially from theatre critics. Many of my fellow actors asked if Rory and Terry would come to *their* press nights.

It was great working at the Young Vic, a full house every night with lots of well-known actors and politicians coming to see the show. At that time the Leader of the Opposition for the Labour party was Neil Kinnock. He came to see the show, along with his wife Glenis, Ian McKellan, (not knighted at the time), and other members of the Labour party. As Sue and I were ardent Labour supporters it was an honour to have them in the audience. They enjoyed the show very much and later invited Sue and myself to dinner at a nearby Italian restaurant. I sat next to Neil and had a great conversation with him on most subjects: theatre, sport, TV, and of course politics. I found him to be a very warm, intelligent man and think he would have made a great Prime Minister given the chance. He understood the man in the street and the struggle of the underprivileged. It's a shame he listened to his spin-doctors and advisers; he should have just been himself when he was giving speeches to the nation. We had a great evening with them and I continued to give my help and services to the Labour party at that time.

A friend of mine from my Liverpool Everyman days, Carl Chase, was in town, working on *Aliens 3* out at Pinewood studios. He invited me onto the set one day to see what a big Hollywood blockbuster was like to work on. He introduced me to some of the crew and I found that the sound-man was a real *Brookside* fan, and he invited me to sit next to him whilst they were filming. So I put on some headphones and watched some of the takes with Sigourney Weaver and Charles Dance. After the shooting had finished, some of the American cast came over to look on the sound guy's monitor to watch playback. They thought I was a new sound assistant, but the soundman put them right, he told them I was an actor in a proper drama, *Brookside*. They didn't know what the hell that was as it wasn't shown in the States. All the cast in *Aliens 3* had shaved heads as it was set on a spacecraft that was a penal colony. I invited them all to come and see 'To' at the Young Vic and they accepted. So that night when we went out on stage we saw a sea of bald heads in the stalls.

I didn't think that the Americans would get 'To' as it was set in the North West of England; I mean that's even foreign to Southerners, and Jim's dialogue is very poetic. I had underestimated the play, however; it was really universal, as the characters were recognisable in any country.

We had been doing the play for over three months now and even though we were loving doing it we were also looking forward to letting it go and moving on to the next project, whatever that may be. 'To' later became 'Two' and went on to be performed all over the country and the world, by different casts, and is now part of our schools syllabus. We didn't know if we were going to get back into television or not, as in the past actors that had been in a soap for too long became typecast and their TV careers tended to be over. So it was a matter of waiting for the phone to ring once we became available again. However before the end of the run of 'To', Sue and I were both offered work on TV dramas - so we didn't wait long.

Sue went off to do a three-part drama for the BBC and I was offered a Screen 2 for BBC 2. The TV film I was offered was called *Thacker*, a supernatural thriller set in the Cotswolds. The director was Richard Spence, a director that I had worked with many times on *Brookside*. He in fact had fulfilled a promise to me: while we were on *Brookside* together, I had asked him if I left Brookside would he employ me if he was working on another project? He told me if the right part came along he would, and he did.

The part I was to play was far removed from my *Brookie* character Billy Corkhill. I was playing a middle class estate agent and my girlfriend was played by Samantha Bond. The whole cast was very high profile. One of my all-time favourites, Lesley Philips was in the cast. It was such a different experience working on a drama like this. You had more time to shoot - instead of trying to cram 12 minutes a day into the camera, 5 would be about the average. You had the luxury of having time to think about what you were doing and saying in a scene. Also Richard the director worked in the way I liked to work which was how I had learnt at drama school: looking at the character you were playing in more depth, giving them a background and a life before this story. Richard also used improvisation to get to the heart of a scene; it was wonderful to work in this way especially in television. This was what I had hoped for when I left Brookside. To be able to get the chance to work with some of our country's leading actors and directors in varied and new projects. In fact it was a very posh cast indeed, not only Samantha Bond and Lesley Philips, but also such esteemed actors as Celia Imrie, Margaret Tyzack, and Graham Crowden. I was feeling a little out of my depth at first. I'd been a soap actor for the past 5 years and here I was mixing with some of the British Acting Aristocracy! I was in makeup with Margaret Tyzack and Samantha Bond and they were discussing their time at the RSC. This was making me feel even more insecure as I could not contribute to the conversation, not having worked at the RSC.

The irony was, I had been offered a place at the RSC just after I had finished doing 'To' at the Young Vic. David Thacker, who was artistic director at the Young Vic at the time, was leaving to join the RSC and asked me if I would like to audition for the part of Launce in *Two Gentlemen of Verona*, the first play he was to direct there. I did the audition and they offered me a season with The Royal Shakespeare Company but I turned it down. It was an 18-month contract and the only decent part I had for that season was Launce. It would have tied me up for too long. Having just finished a long run of 'To' I wasn't ready for another lengthy theatre run and was hoping for more TV work.

Back in the makeup room I overheard Margaret say to Sam how much she loved *Brookside* and wasn't it great to have John McArdle working on this film. I was so chuffed that this wonderful classical actress liked me and my work. I had thought they might be snobby about a Soap actor working alongside them but they were warm, welcoming and lovely to work with, especially Celia Imrie and Stephen Moore.

I was filming very close to Northampton, where I used to live before becoming an actor. I had a day off and decided to take a drive over there to look up some old friends. It was about six years since I had been back so it was hit and miss if anyone I knew would be around. I first went to the estate where I used to live and looked up some of the old neighbours. Most of them were out or at work, but one friend of mine Muhammad Hussein who used to repair my old banger cars, was in. He answered the door and was delighted that I had come to visit him and his family. He invited me in and they couldn't believe that I had become this famous actor in a matter of five years. They were pleased for me and wanted signed photos to prove to their friends that they knew me. I then went back to the College of Further Education where it all started. I met up with Martin Banks, my old Drama tutor and other lecturers that I knew and we had a great night talking over old times. Martin asked me would I come back to college sometime and give a talk about my career, which I did on a later visit.

Then came the wrap party for the end of filming on *Thacker* and it was sad to be saying goodbye to a wonderful cast and crew that I had been working with for the past six weeks. That's the hard part of the job, you make very close friends with people you are working with for a very short time and then you move on and may never work with them again. You never forget them because you have shared so much trust and emotion together. There are some you would never want to work with again ever, but they are few and far between.

I was just getting used to being at home, when my agent rang about a BBC 2 series set in a prison. I was up for the part of Jack Preston, a South London drugs baron, so again a long way from a Scouse electrician. The series was to be directed by Nick Renton and it was produced by Eileen Quinn and Eric Fellner, two really up and coming young producers. I went into the interview, with an attitude of a confident London sophisticated drug lord. The interview went well but they had another actor in mind for the part - Kenneth Cranham, who was a great choice I have to say. A week or two later my agent rang, telling me that Kenneth had turned the part down and it was now on offer to me. This is the way things work in this business – you're not always the first choice, but that doesn't matter as long as you get the job in the end.

The series was called *Underbelly* and all the prison scenes, which I was in, were to be shot in Northern Ireland. The story was not set in Ireland; it was set in London/ Manchester, but the only empty prison available was a woman's prison in South Armagh. I had to do a bit of research on how to play this character, so my first task was to master a south London accent. My first port of call was an actor that I had worked with on *Thacker* a really good young character actor called Steve Sweeney. I went down to London to spend some time with Steve as he was going to help me with the accent. He was a very good teacher and I learnt very quickly. You can go to a voice and dialect coach who is very good at teaching you in a more technical way, but I preferred to learn from a native. Steve invited me to a celebrity football match at the Fulham ground as one of the actors that was going to be in *Underbelly* would be there and we could meet before the filming started. When we got to the venue I saw Ray Winston, who was one of the footballers. I said to Steve that he was one of my favourite actors, and Steve then told me he was the one doing *Underbelly*. He introduced me to Ray and it was a great first meeting. This guy had a great sense of humour, asking me why a Mickey Mouse (slang for Scouse) was playing a South London villain? In fact he would be playing my henchman in the drama.

He took me under his wing, so to speak, Ray gave me some tips on how to play this sort of character. He said that they were not really bruisers; they were more sophisticated and liked nice suits and good wine, and beautiful women. He went through the accent with me, telling me not to open my mouth too wide as that was a more East End accent. Ray was so helpful and generous in helping me build my character. Again I was mixing with an illustrious cast; besides Ray Winston we had David Hayman, Tom Wilkinson and Michael Feast.

Kathy was a little concerned about me working in Northern Ireland as it was at the height of the troubles. People were being assassinated and bombs were being planted throughout the country. As we knew very little about the situation it was somewhat worrying, but I was still adventurous and was looking forward to the series and the excitement of filming in Northern Ireland. The main set was Armagh gaol in South Armagh so we were put up in a hotel in Portadown about eleven miles from the set. The hotel was a modern run-of-the-mill *Holiday Inn* type of building. Most of the cast were put up here and the crew had found some small bed and breakfast places in a small village near Armagh. It was 1991 and mobile phones were not as common as they are now.

At this time we had also found out that Kathy was pregnant again so I went for a walk outside the hotel to find a phone box to give Kathy a call to see how she was and to tell her I had arrived safely and what a nice place it was. I could have used the hotel phone, but that cost a fortune and it was nice to get out. About a quarter of a mile from the hotel along a country road I came across a red phone box. It was such a beautiful day, the sun was shining and the road was quiet with no traffic and just the sounds of the countryside and the birds singing. I got through to Kathy and was telling her how nice I thought Northern Ireland was and how friendly the people were. As I was saying all this, a British Army vehicle pulled up outside the phone box and started setting up a road block. Fully armed soldiers were jumping into ditches and getting into defence positions while other soldiers where setting up the road block. I continued to talk to Kathy as if nothing was happening, as I didn't want to worry her. Outside the phone box an officer was gesticulating for me to *get out of the phone box now*! I told Kathy I had to go, as someone wanted to use the phone. Kathy must have thought I didn't want to talk to her as I had only been talking for about five minutes. I came out of the phone box and the officer apologised and said they were on an operation and the area had to be evacuated. It was so strange seeing a military presence on the streets of somewhere so close to home.

We stayed in the hotel in Portadown for a week and then we moved to the village where the crew were staying, as it was cheaper and there was more going on. The village we moved to was called Moy and a very nice village it was too. We were all spread out in the village at different B&Bs, but I was lucky enough to get a lovely room in Tomneys Bar, and that was only because the landlady was a *Brookside* fan. It was the most hospitable place I had ever been to. The local people made you so welcome and could not do enough for you. I think they liked the idea that a

BBC cast and crew were staying in their village. It was also a mixed village, in the sense that both Protestants and Catholics lived side by side. On one side of a street you would see a Union Jack outside the houses and on the other the Irish tricolour.

Filming was full on. We were in every day from Monday to Saturday and sometimes working from 7am to 7pm depending on how much you had in the scenes. We also partied hard. We would get back from the set and have a shower and something to eat then we would drink until all hours – it was not for the faint hearted. One morning we were on our way to work in a hire car driven by one of the runners. In the car with me was David Hayman and David Keyes. We'd had a rough night so we were wearing sunglasses and had our heads down. Further along the road we were stopped by a RUC road block. One of the officers asked us to wind down the windows, and he looked into the car.

Seeing four blokes wearing sunglasses and looking a bit shady, he said, "Which Paramilitary group are you with?"

"The BBC," replied David Hayman.

"I know you are," he said, then gestured us to move on.

Because the story was set in a prison it meant that we had to have hundreds of extras to play the other inmates. The average age of male prisoners in British prisons is 25 to 29 so they had to recruit 200 young men of that age. It was not an easy task for the casting department, so the job was shared with the production department and security. These departments had to have meetings with councillors and Paramilitary representatives, because the jobs had to be shared equally amongst the Catholic and Protestant population. Once the extras had been contracted they had to make a promise not to cause trouble on set with each other. It was a very precarious situation, 200 young Northern Irish men from opposing sides, working together for the next month, in a prison!

Not only was there a problem casting the local men but also a problem with casting Afro Caribbean men as there were hardly any men of that race living there. One of the runners was asked by the casting department to go into Belfast and find any men of that description and ask them if they wanted any work on a TV series. They came across one guy who was busking in the city, who agreed to join us. The rest of the Afro Caribbean actors had to be hired from London. The only guy they found in Belfast was called Freddie Lee and he was from Chicago, USA.

I got talking to Freddie one day as he would bring his guitar on set and play some blues for us in between takes. I would sometimes accompany him with my blues harp, so we became friends. I asked him how he ended up in Belfast. He told me that he had had an argument with his girlfriend of 20 years, because she wanted to get married and he didn't so she threw him out. He had a little money in the bank and decided to go somewhere in the world he had never been before. He went to the library got out a world map, spread it on the table, took out a pin, closed his eyes and stuck it in the map. He said to himself *wherever the pin lands, that is where I will go.* The pin landed in Belfast, Northern Ireland, a place he had never heard of. He stuck by his promise to himself and bought a one-way ticket to Belfast. He said when he first got off the plane he thought he was in Beirut, there was so much military presence. He had been here for two months and didn't have the fare to go back, that's why he was busking. And there were no black folk in this country, so he was feeling homesick. Freddie was at least earning better money doing the extra work than he was busking.

At the weekend, Tomneys Bar was always packed to the hilt with us, the locals and anyone who was passing through. People were so nice; it was hard to believe there were any troubles happening. I asked Lawrence the landlord how come he never has any problems in his pub? He told me that he had three rules: one, no talking religion; two, no talking politics and three, we only play traditional music. If anyone broke those rules they were barred for life.

There were other pubs in the village and we sometimes used to go to them. One of them I went to on the invite of one of the extras that was about a half mile from Tomneys Bar. I was drinking in there until past midnight, as I was not working the next day and then I set off back to my digs alone. Walking along the lane I saw something in the bushes beside me move, but I thought it must be a cat or something, so I just carried on. Then suddenly whatever it was came out of the bush. I realised it was a young soldier in full camouflage carrying a rifle. He stepped in front of me and asked me where I was going. I told him that I was going back to my digs. Then he said that I looked familiar and told me not to move. He went back into the bush and returned with another soldier. He confirmed to his colleague that I did look familiar and to get the photos to see if I was on the wanted list. The Sergeant came back with the list and looked at me then turned to his men and said, "Idiots, it's Billy Corkhill!"

They apologised to me and asked me what I was doing there telling me I shouldn't be walking along this lane late at night and how dangerous it was. With that, the rest of the squad came out of the bushes and escorted me home. How many people can say they've had a military escort to take them home?

The next day we had the big riot scenes to do. This was such a big set up that if anyone made a mistake – cast or crew – it would take at least three hours to reset. So there was a lot riding on it. The scene started with a riot kicking off in the prison, and meanwhile, my character and David Hayman's character had taken the warden and his male secretary hostage and we had a helicopter coming for us in the prison yard. The first part of the scene was us winding our way through the prison whilst the riot was in progress. Before the start of the scene, Nick Renton, the director, gathered the 200 extras to give them some direction on the riot scene. He told them he wanted it to look real, but not be real. In other words you can smash up what you like and make a huge mess of the place but no harm must come to yourselves or others involved in the scene. One of the extras spoke up, saying "You don't have to tell us about riots" and everyone just fell about laughing, after all these young men had grown up through the troubles.

On *action* we stood behind the camera until the riot was in full swing. After about ten beats we had to make our way through all this flying debris and mayhem. We had dialogue but there was no chance of stopping if you forgot your lines. The distance we had to cover was about 200 metres, a long way in such conditions. We got to the end of the scene without drying or dying and the director shouted *cut*, but the extras didn't hear him. There was so much noise and they were so into what they were doing that they were oblivious to the cameras and the director. Nick shouted *cut* a few more times, then gave up. We waited until they had run out of steam, and then it suddenly stopped. The rest of the cast and crew applauded them on what was one of the best riot scenes ever put on film – and no one got hurt.

The second part of the scene was out in the prison yard with the helicopter. We had our hostages at gunpoint and dragged them across the prison yard to the waiting helicopter. Can you imagine the security checks and liaisons with the security forces and paramilitaries to clear this scene? I mean, guns and helicopters in Northern Ireland during the troubles? The scene went well and we got it done in a day, which was all that was allowed – the cost of the helicopter alone was about £2,000 an hour.

Sadly this job had come to an end and we had a wrap party to end all wrap parties.

The producers did a brilliant job, supplying all the food and booze. Everyone involved in the making of this series was invited. It was held in Tomneys beer garden. Freddie Lee wrote and played us the *Underbelly Blues*. The cast had had a whip round earlier to buy him a ticket home to marry his long-term girlfriend. He gave a speech after he was presented with his air ticket, saying it was the best experience of his life, that he had made some great friends and he would remember it for the rest of his days.

I was glad to get home to see Kathy and Katie, I had missed them so much. This was the longest I had been away from home since I had been acting. After I had been home a couple of weeks, I got a phone call in the early hours of the morning. It was Freddie Lee, ringing to tell me that he had got home safe, he was back with his girlfriend and they were getting married. He invited a few of us over to join him on his wedding day, but because of work commitments none of us could make it. Doing that job changed my outlook on Northern Ireland. Don't get me wrong: it was a mess, the sectarian killings and the divisions amongst the population were real and there was no getting away from that. But we as visitors to NI were made most welcome by both sides of the community. The people went out of their way to keep their troubles to themselves, never involving us once or asking our opinion on the subject, even though it was on our minds at the time.

We found out after we had left Moy, that nearly everyone in that area had someone who had been killed or jailed because of the troubles. But nobody mentioned that to us or asked us to take sides. They were a very dignified and friendly group of people and I would like to thank them for their friendship and hospitality.

When I first arrived in Moy, the room I was staying in had no television and I mentioned this to Margaret the landlady. She said, "Don't worry about that I will get you one."

So she asked around the village to see who had a spare TV and Mrs Keenan from down the road gave me hers. Another time I had rushed out to work because I was running a little late and left my wallet on the bed. I mentioned this to Ray Winston asking him if it might get pinched.

He said, "No chance. They're that friendly over here, when you get back tonight you'll probably have a new music centre and a bottle of whisky in your room."

When I did get home that night, the cleaning lady had put my wallet under my pillow for safekeeping.

This job in Northern Ireland made an impression on me. Not just because I was working on a top BBC drama but because the location was more dramatic in real life than what we were doing on screen. I made so many friends in such a short space of time, gone but not forgotten.

Our son Joseph was born on the 7th March 1992 the same birthdate as my mother which was lovely for her. He had sandy hair and big blue eyes and when he was born he didn't cry, he just looked around the room as if weighing everything up. Katie was now ten and had to get used to this new little brother. She was a great little helper to Kathy when I was away working. She was a lovely little girl – quite shy and timid but a loving, sensitive and kind child, qualities she has kept as a young woman. Joseph was always full of energy with an inquisitive nature and a love of life which he has to this day. All three of my kids have a wonderful sense of humour, get on with each other and are great fun to be around. I feel at my happiest when we get the chance to all spend time together.

I must admit I do prefer TV and film to the theatre; it suits my style of acting more. I like to be as natural as possible and you can do that in front of a camera because it picks up the subtlest of facial expressions and you can speak in a normal way. In theatre it is much harder; you have to project that realism to the back of a huge auditorium and that takes a lot of technical skill. Also TV and film pays better: you may only have to do three or four TV jobs a year to earn a decent living, whereas in theatre you would have work all year to earn the same. It was good to have breaks in between TV jobs, though, because you were away from home, and if you had a month or two off work you could spend it with the family. I was also gaining more confidence as an actor with each new job, working on high calibre projects and enjoying myself.

One of my most memorable Screen Two films for the BBC was called *Skallagrigg*, based on the 1987 novel written by William Horwood and influenced by Horwood's relationship with his own daughter Rachel, who has cerebral palsy. The main cast were to be played by young disabled actors. This would be my first experience of working with actors who had a disability. The director was Richard Spence, a brilliant man who I had worked with before. Richard was very thorough in his work as I mentioned earlier. We actually had a week's rehearsal, a luxury in film making. We had a very talented young cast of unknowns, and for some of them this was their first taste of film work. They would be supported by an exemplary cast: Bernard

You Never Said Goodbye

Hill, Billy Whitelaw, Kevin Wheatley, and Richard Briers. The lead was an actress called Kerry Noble who had cerebral palsy. I had no knowledge of this condition and didn't know what to expect from the actors I was working with. I was soon to find out.

After the read through we all had a coffee and chatted about the script. I told some of the young actors who had never done any filming before to ask me or any of the other experienced actors if they had any questions about acting in front of the camera. Kerry Noble asked me if I ever watch myself on television when a programme is aired. I replied that I did but I didn't like it. Then a young actor said " *Neither do we.*"! That young actor was a very bright and funny guy called Jamie Bedard, 23 years old and with cerebral palsy. He was difficult to understand at first as his speech was impaired by his condition, but after a while I began to tune in and understand him, and found him to be mischievous, witty and fun to work with. We became good friends and worked well together considering I was playing his abuser in the film. Working with these young actors was a real education for me in terms of understanding the difficulties of people with disabilities and also their sense of fun and humour in spite of these difficulties. The filming days were long and hard and some of it was very harrowing because of the nature of the story but these guys never complained and were true professionals.

I actually met and got drunk with one of my musical heroes, Ian Drury, who was also in the film – he was such a great bloke and it was great fun to be in his company. Nearly all the actors were in the hotel bar one night, having a great time and getting slowly pissed. At about 2am they shut the bar and everyone had to make their way to their rooms. Ian Drury looked across at me and said "As you're the only one with use of all your limbs you've been allocated as our carer. You need to help us all to our rooms."

Well that was a job and a half, trying to get wheelchairs and walking frames belonging to eight very drunk disabled people into a lift. Plus, I was in a pretty drunken state myself. We eventually all crammed into the lift and staggered to our rooms, but I think it took about an hour to do so. This film was critically acclaimed and went on to win a BAFTA for Best Drama.

My next job was a three-part drama for the BBC, called *Gallowglass* and based on a novel by Ruth Rendell writing as Barbara Vine. As I was a fan of Ruth Rendell it was such a thrill to be playing one of her characters. It was directed by an ex-*Brookside* director called Tim Fywell, an excellent guy to work with. When he was watching a scene behind the camera, you could see he was playing all the characters; he was so involved with the story. It also had an excellent cast: Paul Rhys, Claire Hackett, Arkie Whiteley and a young Michael Sheen. It was shot in the Cotswolds and set mostly on a country estate – a dream job. I was getting used to this lifestyle, staying in posh hotels and having a car pick you up for work. Picking up scaffolding tubes on an ice-cold morning in Northampton seemed a long way away. But after ten weeks of filming it was again great to get home, not matter how luxurious it was.

Just when I thought it couldn't get much better I landed a part opposite Julie Walters in a film for the BBC called *Bambino Mio*, filming in London, France and South America. Unfortunately I didn't film in South America but I did film in Chablis, north-west Burgundy. It was my first foreign location and I was so excited. In fact I always get excited about travelling abroad, as I love travel. The difference here was that I was being paid to travel and to do something that I love doing; it doesn't get much better than that. Working with Julie was a hoot – she is such a lovely actress and a wonderful person.

We were filming in a restaurant in the centre of London. It was a long scene between us and it was going to take most of the day, with lots of dialogue and lots of camera set-ups. I have always been a great fan of Julie's, especially the work she did with Victoria Wood. Her characters were so good and so funny. I got talking to her about this and she asked me which my favourite one was. There were so many I found it difficult to choose, but I told her the old waitress delivering the soup to the table was one of my favourites. A while later we were filming part of a scene where Julie's character leaves the table to answer an important phone call. This shot would be of her returning to the table with the good news she had received. On *action*, Julie leaves the phone and heads back to the table to join me but she does so as the old woman delivering the soup, staggering to the table where I am sitting and saying *Two soups?* Needless to say the crew and I plus all the extras were in stitches.

We flew to Chablis to film some scenes in a chateau with a vineyard attached. The village of Chablis is so beautiful, a real picturesque French village. I remember walking around it after dinner one evening and thinking how lucky I was. When you film abroad it is usually only the key people that go, i.e. main actors, director, DOP and the designer. The rest of the crew are recruited locally. Of course we had French caterers and they were superb, but the difference between the British and French caterers was the French served wine at lunchtime. Although this is a real treat it affects your work after lunch so I had to knock that on the head the next day. I left Chablis with a case of the Vintner's best Chablis as a gift – perk of the job.

I next saw Julie in Ireland. I was on holiday with my family in Dunmore East and I noticed a film crew in town. They were filming an Alan Bleasdale series called *Jake's Progress*. I couldn't get away from film crews even on my holidays. In fact I bumped into some people I had worked with on other jobs. They told me Julie Walters was in it and that she was in her Winnebago. I was with Kathy, Katie and baby Joseph, so I knocked on her Winnie and she was so pleased to see me. She invited us all in and we sat with her for a while talking about family and how she missed her little girl. It was lovely to see her again. This business can be like being in one big family; you make friends very quickly in a short space of time and share so much with them on an emotional level, that when you meet up again years later you just pick up where you left off.

Henry

It was December the 28th, 1995 a date that is etched on the memories of everyone in our family.

Your lovely grandson, Henry, tragically passed away at the tender age of two and a half. Henry was Rory and Jackie's only son and who they cherished and adored. He was a happy cheerful little fella that made you smile whenever you were in his company. Even though Rory and Jackie were separated at the time, they were still good friends and they still shared their mutual love for Henry. Rory lived in Amersham and Jackie lived with Henry in Plymouth, her home town. Rory would visit his son regularly and loved him dearly. They had tried hard to have children for a while, so when Henry was born he was very special indeed. So you can imagine his early death was devastating to them both. It was during the Christmas holidays, a time for children and families. I received a phone call in the middle of the night from Mum sobbing down the phone, barely able to speak. When she did manage to talk she told us that Henry had died that night, very suddenly of meningitis. Kathy and I were so shocked. We couldn't believe it. It's so much harder to take in when it's a child that dies so young. It's not the natural order of things.

We had to be with my family at this awful time, so we dropped the kids off with Walter and Joan, Kathy's parents, then drove to Liverpool to pick up Mum and Sharon. We then took the long, seemingly endless drive to Plymouth, where great sadness was awaiting us.

On our arrival at Jackie's house, it was difficult to go inside and face the awful truth of what had happened. The rest of my family were already there, consoling and giving their much needed support to Rory and Jackie. I went to my brother and had no words to say to him. I just hugged him. There was nothing I could say or do that would bring his son back. He was in bits, in a state of disbelief and wondering why. Jackie seemed stronger; she was telling us about Henry's passing. I think she was in a state of shock and this was her way of coping with it. She also has a strong faith and this was probably helping her. Rory wanted to know why a loving God could do such a thing, take his young son who had just started his life and was innocent to the world. Rory also wanted to know what the doctors had done to save Henry, not that he was blaming anyone, he just wanted to know. I had to admire him for this; he wanted questions answered as to why Henry had been taken from him.

Rory asked me to accompany him to go and see Henry at the Chapel of Rest. I was honoured that he asked me even though I knew it was going to be heartbreaking. On arriving at the chapel we were told to wait outside while they went to get Henry's body. We were then told to go into the chapel to see him. That moment has never left me to this day, seeing my little nephew lying there so still, like a little angel asleep, then looking at my poor grieving brother falling apart before my eyes. It was the saddest moment of my life.

We then had the funeral to attend, which was going to be so hard, our final goodbye to this beautiful boy. The church was packed with friends, family and neighbours who wanted to pay their respects. His little white coffin arrived and that was the realisation that this little lad was leaving us for good. I know this will sound like a cliché, but there was not one dry eye in that church. It was the saddest funeral that I had ever been to. Kathy sang *Away in a Manger* and I read out a version of WH Auden's *Stop the Clocks* that was adapted by our brother Terry. We left Rory and Jackie on their own to say their final goodbyes to Henry. We went home after a couple of days, leaving Rory and Jackie to their sadness. On getting home and seeing my own kids I realised how precious they were to me and how lucky I was to have them.

In the aftermath of Henrys death, Rory found out more about meningitis and why it took Henry. He decided to fundraise for the Meningitis Research Foundation. He organised a football match, with his own team playing against an all-star celebrity team to raise money. We got such tremendous support from actors I had worked with and some pro footballers. The actors that turned up to play for Rory's game included Ray Winstone, Perry Fenwick, Dougray Scott, Sue Johnston, Mickey Starke, Sean Dingwall, and Sam Kane. After the football match we had an evening do and Vinny Jones turned up to do the auction for us. He had travelled up from Southampton that day after playing a match and did a great job for us with the auction, raising quite a lot of money. The day was a huge success and it raised more than £10,000.

The effect of Henry's death on Rory took its toll on him. Before Henry died, Rory ran and managed a very successful chip shop in Little Chalfont, Bucks. It was very popular with the locals, as was he. He would get celebrities coming to the shop to buy their weekend fish supper, people such as Ozzie Osbourne and Liam Gallagher. When Rory came back from Plymouth, he lost interest in the business and tended to drink more and become depressed. I can't even imagine how you cope with losing your only son. The pain he and Jackie suffered – and still do suffer is unimaginable. Even 18 years later the Christmas period is a reminder of that terrible day.

Rory is doing well now with the help of his lovely partner Andrea, who has stood by him and looked after him through some very dark days. He has a good job with the post office and he still raises money for the Meningitis Research Foundation. In fact, Dad, he is the more like you: sporty, tough, headstrong, argumentative, and sometimes he can be a bit of a hothead. But beneath that macho man lies a sensitive soul. He writes moving and intelligent poetry, and does have a gift for writing. He has been very supportive of me in my career and is a loyal brother. In fact all members of my family have been supportive of my acting, not just when I became well known for my television work, but when I was starting out.

I think at first they thought I was mad going into a profession that was precarious and unknown: *our John an actor?* They knew I was taking it seriously when I went to drama school and when they came to see *Lennon* at the Everyman Theatre in Liverpool. It's funny, really: I left Liverpool in 1969 to seek fame and fortune abroad; little did I know it was right here on my doorstep. My first step into full time rep theatre started at the Everyman and my first television break was *Brookside* – both in my hometown. I have in fact played all the major theatres in Liverpool; besides the Everyman, I have worked at the Playhouse, the Empire, and given talks on drama at the Unity Theatre. Also, the film I wrote and directed, *The Duke* premiered at the Royal Philharmonic in Hope Street. So my reconnecting to this wonderful city was a success and I am proud to be part of that cultural legacy.

A great thing about getting regular TV work is that you can afford a holiday somewhere exotic, once a year. But getting the holiday planned is a different thing altogether. You can't book anything in advance as you don't know when your next job will start, so you have to take it at the last minute, which in those days meant taking the kids out of school and dropping all other appointments. Also we used to take holidays in destinations which weren't as popular with the British tourists. I couldn't go to places like Benidorm or Tenerife, because I wouldn't get a moment's peace. Even though I had left *Brookside* some five years previously, the British TV viewers have good memories and to them I was still Billy Corkhill.

On one occasion we went to Malta for a couple of weeks. We went out of season hoping it would be quiet without many English holiday makers around. I was so wrong. A guy on the journey out there asked me to have photos taken with him and his kids, which I did quite happily. After all it's the public who watch your work and if you're prepared to put yourself in people's living rooms two or three times a week, then you should expect some attention when you're out and about. But on this occasion, Malta being a very small island, we kept bumping into this man and his family. Because I was friendly to him on the first day, he now thought I was his best friend, wanting more pictures and asking if we wanted to eat with them, when all we wanted to do was chill out and enjoy our holiday. So whenever we caught sight of this chap, we would end up hiding in shop doorways or taking a detour to avoid him. Once we were on the ferry from mainland Malta to the island of Gozo and he was on the same ferry, so there was no getting away from him. Kathy was struggling through a doorway with the children and a pushchair when the man approached. She thought he was going to help her but he just shouted at her "Where is he?! Where is he?!" and when she told him she didn't know (and that she wished she bloody knew!) he just ran off and left her to struggle. I think I got into trouble over that one!

One of my all-time favourite holidays was in Tuscany. Such beautiful unspoilt countryside, with its terracotta roofed houses and medieval buildings and the food, the culture and the Italian way of life was something to be cherished. So after Nice, Tuscany was my favourite part of the world. In the summer of '96 we booked an expensive holiday to Greece and I had to pay up front, so crossed my fingers that no work would come up during that period.

My agent rang and told me that Granada TV had been on and wanted to see me for a major part in *Prime Suspect 5*. He gave me the dates and of course they clashed with this expensive holiday. I had been a great fan of the *Prime Suspect* series and of course, Helen Mirren, so this job was very high on my want-to-do list. It was to be directed by Phil Davis and produced by Gub Neil. This was a dream of a job. The interview went well and I came away hoping it would be mine. The next day, Dennis, my agent, rang and gave me the good news, saying that filming would be starting in two weeks time. So that was the holiday cancelled although they did agree to refund half my money when I explained why, so that was something. Although I don't think my family were too impressed at the time.

Working with Helen Mirren was something I was really looking forward to. I had admired her work for such a long time and now I would be working closely with her. My character was DCS Martin Ballinger, head of Manchester Serious Crime. Helen's character Jane Tennison was working on my team, and I would be her boss and her lover - like I say, it was a dream job. I first met Helen at the read-through in Manchester and liked her straight away; she was warm, friendly and such a professional. There were quite a few young actors in this series and after the read-through Helen took the floor and said to these young actors that if it was their first time working in front of a camera, that they should ask any questions about the technical side of our work. They were not to be afraid to ask any member of the crew or cast if they were unsure about jargon or anything they didn't understand. I was so impressed by this - it's so often taken for granted that you know everything about acting in front of a camera just because you're an actor.

Our first day of filming was in the majestic Manchester Town Hall, and they couldn't have picked a worse day to start filming. It was May 11th 1996, and Liverpool, my beloved team, were playing Manchester United in the FA Cup Final - so my mind was going to be in two places. My first scene in the morning was in the main conference hall, due to take most of the morning. After lunch it was my first scene with Helen; in fact it was the first time the two characters had met on screen. I was a little nervous working with this great actress, but tried not to show it. Consequently, I think I must have come across rather cool at the beginning. The match had kicked off and a group of supporting artistes had found a television in one of the rooms and they were watching the football with some members of the crew. So in between takes I would disappear into this room to catch up on the match. It took about twenty minutes to reset so I had plenty of time. Usually when you start work with someone new you spend the set up times together, discussing the scene etc. I must have come across as very rude disappearing for the twenty or thirty minutes.

When I came back to do some more filming Helen asked: "Where do you go in between set ups?"

I apologised, explaining the importance of the game and why I seemed to be ignoring her. She asked if she could join me.

"Of course, as long as you shout for Liverpool," I said.

She came into the TV room and the extras couldn't believe Helen Mirren sitting down with them to watch the footy. Unfortunately, we got beat one-nil that day.

I learned a lot working with Helen. She was a true professional, and she cared so much about the programme. After all it was her show and the past four series were of a high standard and were a huge success. Helen would work on the script herself in the evenings and the next day she would give me the changes and although it was a pain re-learning them, she was usually right – they were better because of her input.

The great thing about filming in Manchester was I could go home every night and see the family. Towards the end of the filming, Helen and I had a very difficult and long scene to shoot. It was the last scene of the day and we were running late. We went back to our Winnebagos until they had finished lighting. They then called us on set to shoot the scene. When we got on set they informed us that they were not quite ready and if we didn't mind waiting they wouldn't be too long. So we sat and waited and waited.

After about half an hour Helen got up off her seat and shouted, "How much longer are you going to be? You've got two actors here going off the boil, with 20 minutes before we wrap, so no pressure on us!"

Within two minutes it was lit and we did the scene in two takes. Helen was right: you can wait for lighting to set up for an hour or so, yet you have to perform in minutes. I know lighting is important and makes the look of the film, but the performance is what tells the story.

I must say making *Prime Suspect 5* was hard work but I loved every minute of it. My career was on a great level, I was working with some of the country's best actors and the quality of programmes I was doing was of a very high standard. I wondered if things could get any better than this.

The Place of the Dead

The next job I was to embark on would take me back to Australia and then on to Borneo to climb Mount Kinabalu.

In 1994, an army expedition had set out to abseil from Mount Kinabalu into Lowes Gully but it had gone disastrously wrong. Jeff Pope had written and produced a film about this expedition. It was to be directed by Suri Krishnamma and included in the cast were Greg Wise, Timothy West, Dougray Scott, Simon Dutton, Ralph Brown and Dave Nellist. Basically the story was about the two British Army officers leading the group of eight soldiers on an expedition into Lowes Gully in Borneo. I was to play one of the officers, a Major Ron Foster and Simon Dutton was to play Lt Colonel Robert Neil.

To prepare us for the filming in the rainforest in Brisbane and the Kinabalu Mountain, Suri the director and Jeff the producer arranged for the cast to spend a weekend on a military style survival course in the Cotswolds. This is where the cast would meet for the first time and bond together before embarking on what was to be a gruelling film schedule. The course consisted of team building, survival techniques and physical endurance. The course was run by ex-SAS and Para NCOs and they were there to put us through our paces. The first part of the day consisted of team work and problem solving. In the afternoon we went for a 10k run with full back packs, it was just like being back in the Paras. In fact, one of the tutors reminded me of you, Dad, his name was Jack and he was ex-APTC – a real ball breaker.

We ended the day knowing a little more about one another. We slept out in the open that night and it was early November, so not much sleep. We were woken at 5.30am by the trainers shouting at us to get our *prissy little actor's arses* up and swim across the lake that was just yards away from where we were sleeping. The lake was about 200 metres across. I dived in and the shock of the ice cold water hit me straight away. I started to swim like mad just to get out of this freezing cold water. Halfway across the lake I thought I had cramp and panic nearly kicked in. Jack was swimming alongside of me and told me to keep going and if I was to get in real trouble he would signal for a boat to come and get me. I was 45, and thought to myself, *I shouldn't be doing this sort of thing at my age*. I just kept going, and in fact I was way ahead of many younger members of the cast. I reached the other side and dragged myself out of the lake. My body was red with cold, teeth chattering like castanets. We ran to the hot showers and felt very relieved and proud of our achievement. We were then taken out into the forest to learn how to capture small game animals, skin them, clean them, cook them, and eat them. Hopefully we would have caterers on the real job though! At the end of the course we had a celebration of beers in the hot tub and a run down on how we had done. Jack thought for a bunch of 'Nancy boy actors' we did very well.

We had a month off before we departed for Australia, so it was great to spend that time at home with Kathy and the children. This would be the longest I would be away from them, as the filming would take three months. I have been very lucky that I have never had to do long theatre tours or pantomimes as many actors with families have to do. An actor I know who had five children gave up working on tours, after coming home for the weekend after a long tour. It was 4 am and his 5year old son got up and came into the kitchen as he got in. His little boy looked up at him then shouted up the stairs to his mother, *Mummy there's a man in the kitchen*. So it was going be hard for Kathy on her own with the children and me half way across the world.

The time came for me to make my journey to Australia and my family saw me off at the station, which was quite tearful. I was looking forward to seeing Australia again and especially as we were going to Brisbane and it was an area I hadn't been to before. On arrival in Brisbane we were taken to our 5-star hotel on Queensland's Gold Coast. After costume fittings, make up calls and a meeting with the producers and director, we were free for a couple of days before we started shooting in the rainforests on Tambourine Mountain. We were using the rainforests in Brisbane as opposed to Borneo, where the story is set, because of cost and convenience to amenities. This meant we would film in the jungle in the daytime and return to our hotels in the evening. It was wonderful returning to a luxury hotel after spending ten hours in a hot sweaty jungle. We had the weekends off so, we used to swim, sightsee and socialise with some of the Aussie crew. Timothy West celebrated his 60th birthday with us. We went to a night club later and they wouldn't let Timothy in because he was wearing jeans and trainers, so we went back to the hotel to finish off the evening.

The crew we had were mostly Australian, but our first assistant director was British. He had been in the business for about 35 years and had worked mainly in LA on Hollywood movies, so he was a very experienced and a top class first assistant to the director. One day we were shooting a scene between myself, Simon Dutton and Dougray Scott. In the scene, Dougray's character had just run down the mountain to inform us that he was going to go ahead with his team into the gully. It was a simple enough scene: Dougray runs into where we are camped and we have about two pages of dialogue. We rehearse the scene and the First Assistant asks if everyone is ready to shoot the scene quickly as we were running out of time. Everyone is ready. He then informs make up to apply some sweat to Dougray as he is supposed to have just run down a mountain. When the makeup girl approaches Dougray he asks her what she's doing. She tells him the first asked her to apply some false sweat. Dougray says no, he will create some real sweat by running around for a few seconds, thus being out of breath and making it more realistic (in fact it was something I would have done myself so you don't have to act it).

The first assistant went ballistic. He turned to Dougray and said, "We haven't got time for all that method shit, just get the fucking make up on and do the scene'.

We couldn't believe what we had just heard and neither could Dougray.

He turned to the First and said, "You do your job and I'll be the actor, ok?"

We all just stood watching this standoff between them.

Suri was about to say something when the First completely lost it saying, "I've had enough of this method shit. I've been working in the States for the past ten years and that's all they do and it takes forever to shoot a scene, so you can all fuck off."

Having said that he marched off into the jungle cursing to himself. There was a long silence, then Suri turned to the 3rd assistant and told him he was promoted to first for the rest of the day. We carried on and got the scene in on time doing it the way Dougray wanted. Then as we were leaving we heard this crashing sound coming from the jungle, and all of a sudden the First Assistant appeared. He had been lost for the past hour.

"How the fuck do you get out of this place?"

This was just the beginning; this job was going to be full of real life drama.

John McArdle

We had a long weekend off and a few of us decided to fly to Sydney for the weekend and look up some of my old stomping grounds. So Dave Nellist, Ralph Brown and I flew to Sydney after work on Friday night. It had been twenty years since I had been in Sydney, so it was going to be interesting to see what had changed in all that time. We landed at about 10 o'clock in the evening with no pre-booking of a hotel. We got a taxi to Kings Cross as this was where the night life never stopped. We had a few beers and took in the denizens of the night, street walkers, drug dealers and drunks. A perfect place for an actor to observe the darker side of human life.

I was getting nostalgic now. It was about 2am and I wanted to go to Bondi and see how much that had changed. So we got a cab to Bondi. We needed to get a hotel as we were knackered after working since 6am that morning. The only hotel that was open was The Bondi Beach Hotel, it was a flea pit twenty years ago and was an even worse flea pit now, but we had no choice. We shared a room at the grand price of $40, the wallpaper peeling off and the pipes making the most annoying groaning sound. It was as hot as hell with no air conditioning and needless to say we didn't get much sleep.

Still, the next morning was a typical Bondi hot, sunny day. I took the lads round to where I used to live, just off the sea front on Lamrock Avenue; someone had graffitied a letter G onto the street name making it Glamrock Avenue. The place hadn't changed in all those years, in fact the whole of Bondi hadn't changed. It was still the same slightly tatty at the edges kind of place, with its 1930s buildings needing a coat of paint and the residents mainly young, surfer, student types. It still had that lovely smell of the sea and sound of the surf that made me think back to when I spent two years of my young life in this area. The rest of the day we spent in and around Sydney, one of the most beautiful cities in the world. We spent another night there and then flew back to Brisbane.

On the last day of filming in Queensland we had a little studio work to do, so a taxi was going to pick some of us up to shoot some pick-up scenes. The cab pulled up outside the hotel and there was already a passenger in the back. I jumped in next to this person who was so big he nearly took up the whole of the back seat. He was huge.

He put out his hand to me and introduced himself. "Hi there, mate, I'm Joe Bugner."

Joe Bugner dad, the ex-British and Commonwealth heavyweight champion who had put up a good fight against your favourite boxer Muhammad Ali. What was he doing in our taxi that morning? It turned out that some of the boys had been out drinking the night before and got talking to him and had invited him onto set this morning. It was a special treat to meet one of our top boxers close up.

After three and a half weeks of filming the jungle scenes in Queensland, we set off on the second leg of our journey to Borneo, to film the mountain scenes. We arrived in Kuala Lumpur at around 10.30pm and checked into one of the most luxurious hotels I have ever stayed in. The foyer of this hotel was palatial, the size of a football field. It had grand art hanging from the ceiling and a pianist playing Mozart, the staff were dressed in Armani and our rooms were suites that backed onto a golf course. All I can say is they must have had a good deal because the budget was not that good. Dougray, Ralph and Dave and I jumped in a cab and asked the driver to take us to where he would eat as it was now 12am and all the restaurants were probably shut. The driver took us down to a market in the middle of town where all the locals gathered to eat and drink. It was very busy for this time of night, but we got a table outside as it was hot and humid. I had one of the best meals ever and it cost us next to nothing. We then went on to a night club so we could have a drink. The club was mainly full of young local people and they were the politest clubbers I have ever come across. They had such good manners and informed us about their city, where to go and which areas to avoid. They even ordered us a taxi to take us back to our hotel at the end of the evening. After three days of the life of luxury we left our beautiful hotel on the next leg of the journey to Borneo. After landing at Kota Kinabalu we set off in a small coach to our next destination, the village of Kinabalu at the foot of the mountain.

The hotel we were going to be staying in for the next three weeks was the opposite of the last one; it was built in the seventies and looked it. There was no air con and the heat was unbearable. The electricity was always going off and some of the guys were stuck in the lift for nearly an hour one day. That's when I decided to use the stairs all the time, which also got me fit for what was to come. I had a room on the fifth floor and had a fantastic view of Mount Kinabalu. It looked so big and awesome; it was intimidating but also challenging in a way. Although the hotel was a little on the *Fawlty Towers* side, the staff were great and besides we wouldn't be spending much time in it as in a few days we would be off filming on the mountain for a week.

To get us and the camera equipment up to the base camp we were to be taken by helicopter, but as the chopper was only a four seater we had to be taken up in stages. I was in the last stage, along with Ralph Brown, an older Chinese actor called John Alansu and one of the wardrobe girls. Our turn came to go up the mountain in the helicopter. All went well until we got close to landing, then the mist came in very quickly and the pilot said he couldn't land in these conditions. So he had to take us back to the bottom of the mountain and wait for the mist to clear. We reached the bottom and decided we would walk up to the base camp, it may take us three or four hours but we could do it. It was a warm day and I was wearing a T shirt and jeans, not the ideal gear for walking up mountains but I thought I'd be ok. After all I was quite fit and felt I could make it to camp Laban Rata without much problem. We also had plenty of water.

The start of the walk was quite easy, but further on it started to get steeper and harder. I was trying to prove to myself how fit I was so was probably taking too fast a pace to sustain for the whole time. After about 8,000 feet, the air was getting thinner and a little cooler, but I was still warm as I was walking fast. After a while I started to feel a little weird and light headed, probably due to the altitude. At one point I felt so exhausted that when I sat down for a rest I didn't want to get up again. I just wanted to lay there and go to sleep. John the Chinese guy told me to get up and keep walking as we had not far to go. So he helped me up and I carried on for the last few miles. We walked into the main camp building to the cheers of all the guys and girls that had been taken up by helicopter. They had drinks for everyone and wanted to celebrate, but I was feeling really bad. I started to shake and feel dizzy. Greg Wise noticed this and said I should go to my bunk and that he would find the medic and get him to come and see me. Some of the guys helped me to my bunk and one of them stayed with me until the medic came.

The medic came with Suri the director, who was very concerned about my situation. The medic wasn't much good really; he didn't even take my temperature or blood pressure, just said that I was tired and gave me some paracetamol. Suri wasn't satisfied about this diagnosis and went on to ask Greg Wise, who has done plenty of outdoor pursuits and mountaineering. Greg thought I had hypothermia, because I was shivering and cold. Greg made a decision to bring my temperature up by using body heat from himself and some of the other actors. As my feet and arms were cold, they pressed their bodies against those areas to try and bring my temperature back to its normal level. It must have worked because after a couple of hours I started to feel better.

The next day I was still confined to my bed. The guys were so attentive, coming in every hour or so to check on me and to see if I needed anything. That night the producer came to see me to ask me if I could go to the summit the next day to film the Lows Gully scenes. I said if I felt better I would. In the film business you don't want to let anyone down – you have a lot of pressure put on you, and as one of the main cast I felt obliged to work, even though I felt on death's door. Stupid I know, but I don't think in

John McArdle

my 34 years as an actor I have ever had a day off through illness. Suri was furious with the producer for putting me in that position. Suri told me that if I was still unwell he would find a way around the filming or he would postpone for a day or two. The next morning I was feeling a whole lot better and told Suri I would be ready to do the scenes on the summit. I was not the only one in the company that was ill, though: one of the Chinese actors had altitude sickness and had to go back down the mountain, and some key members of the crew were also suffering from this illness. The lighting cameraman was one, the sound engineer another as well as the first assistant. They were replaced by their assistants. They must have felt bad because this was the most important part of the film, the top of Mount Kinabalu at sunrise.

We set off about lunch time to reach another small cabin that was just a few kilometres from the summit. We reached the cabin in the late afternoon and went to bed early because we had to set off from there at 2am to reach the top of the mountain in time for sunrise. The cabin itself was your typical mountain log cabin measuring about 15ft by 15ft with five sets of three-tier bunk beds. It had a log stove in the centre and a window either side. I was on one of the top bunks next to Craig Shai Hee, one of the Chinese actors. When the lamps were turned off it was pitch black in the cabin.

At about midnight I awoke to what sounded like someone munching on a bag of crisps. I put my head torch on to see who the midnight muncher was. To my horror I saw two of the largest rats I have ever seen in my life, about the size of a large cat. I immediately woke up Craig, but it didn't seem to bother him, he just rolled over and went back to sleep. By this time most of the cast and crew had woken up and all head torches were on these two gigantic rats. Some of the girls were screaming and so was I inside! I hate rats. One of the Aussie crew threw his boots at them, but this didn't deter the rats one bit, they just kept on eating the food that had been left on the table. The brave Aussie got up and forced them out of the hut through the window where they came in. The window had a pane missing, which is how they'd got in, so the Aussie guy placed some cardboard against the window to prevent them coming back. We all settled back down to sleep.

I was just dropping off to sleep when I heard a scraping sound coming from the window – they were on their way back in for more food. I shouted to the Aussie guy to help again but he just grunted and went back to sleep. The rats got back in and because the food had been put away, they went to look for it, running all around the cabin. I heard lots more screaming and shouting. These horrible beasts were running up and down the bunks looking for food. Even though I was quite warm I just zipped up my sleeping bag to the top, right over my head. We still had two hours before we set off to the top, but I never slept a wink listening to the rats and feeling them run over me – it was a bloody nightmare. Thank God 2am came; the rats had given up by then and buggered off home.

It was a lot colder now and we got dressed and set off to Lowes Gully. We reached the top before sunset so the cameraman was able to set up for the first scene of the day. And what a scene it was. Just as the sun was rising, the expedition team were filmed walking on the summit with this beautiful sunrise behind them. We spent the next four hours filming up there and what a great experience it was. I know it's not the highest mountain in the world, but it felt like it when you were up there. We were above the clouds, but we could still see the South China Sea and Cambodia to the front and the Philippines to the right – what a view. We spent another two days filming at the base camp, then descended the mountain on foot. It's so much easier going down – in fact we ran most of the way. After a great wrap party in Kuala Lumpur (where we chucked the producer into the pool fully clothed!) we headed for home where I was able to spend some quality time with my family who had missed me a lot. Joseph was a little shy of me at first. He was only young and I think he wondered who I was at first. He soon came round especially when he saw the crocodile shaped hat and other gifts I'd brought back for him!

We were able to finish some pick up scenes in Hebden Bridge where they had found some rock face that resembled that of Mount Kinabalu. As Hebden Bridge wasn't far from where we lived Kathy was able to meet some of the cast when we all met for a wrap party meal.

The Duke

This experience of walking up a mountain had a real effect on me. Although I had a rough time with hypothermia and exhaustion I appreciated the beauty and achievement of conquering this tall stretch of land. So after I had been back for a couple of weeks, I decided to do some hill walking in the Lake District, which is not too far from where I live. I think it's the best exercise you can get. You're climbing up hills and mountains in fantastic surroundings with beautiful landscapes, and it's free. You can do it with groups of people or on your own. When I'm walking on my own I let my mind wander and think about all the people who have walked this land before me and it helps me to keep my imagination going and be creative.

It was on one of these walks that I conjured up a story about when I thought my grandad was John Wayne. I told you earlier that after seeing John Wayne in a cowboy picture, I thought he looked like my grandad, and he'd told me he was and I'd believed him. About two months after this walk I was working on a series and pitched my story to an actor I was working with who had done some writing. He thought it was a good story and that I should write a short film about it. So with that encouragement I set out to write a short film about my grandad being John Wayne. I finished my script after about three weeks. It was thirty pages long, which in film time is about half an hour, probably a bit long for a short film. I showed the script to Kathy and she liked it and encouraged me to show it to a producer or director. In fact I did nothing with it and put it in a drawer and forgot about it.

My next job was working on a pilot for a feature film called *Fanny and Elvis*, written and directed by Kay Mellor. It had a great cast including Jenny Agutter and Peter Howitt. During a break in filming I was talking to one of Kay's daughters and told her about my idea for a short film. She thought it was great and told her mother about my script. Kay asked to read it. I was very reluctant to let such a well-known writer read my first draft, but I thought it was worth it as she could tell me if it was rubbish or not. Kay read my script over a weekend. When she came back to work on the Monday she told me she really liked my script and that it would make a great short film, but with some editing as it was too long. Kay agreed to edit my film script for me. She eventually cut it down to about 15 minutes. Although she had cut what I thought were some of my best lines, the script was so much better and tighter.

So now I had a script but no idea about how to go about making a short film and with no money? I was doing a reading at The Script Factory in London. Lots of people from the film business attend these readings, looking for new projects and to do a bit of networking. I got talking to a young producer about my short film and she seemed really interested. She asked if she could read a copy and that she would get back to me if she liked it. The very next day she phoned me to say that she loved the script and that she would produce it for me if I wanted to do it. I was so flattered that she wanted to produce my film and so Sara Proudfoot Clinch became the producer of my short film, entitled *The Duke*.

Sara was just starting out as a producer and wanted to get some more films on her portfolio. She thought mine was going to be a good one to have on it. This short film was going to take about three months in all from start to finish, so I had to inform my agent that I would be unavailable for that period. As Producer, Sara was responsible for raising the money to make the movie, employing the crew, doing deals for post-production and attending festivals. It was a hell of a job so she had to be good. My job as Director was to cast the film, choose my Director of Photography and First Assistant, decide on the look of the film and of course direct it. All my years of working in television would help in my debut as a director. It was still a daunting task though. Sara was a bundle of fire and energy; she had this 'get things done' attitude which was just what was needed for the job ahead. The film was going to be shot on location in Liverpool, so we had to set up a production office there but it needed to be free. Sara managed to get us some office space at the North West Film commission in Bold Street. My son Justin joined us as an associate producer at the tender age of 27. It was so good having him around. He was so good at his job and I loved working with him.

I was supported by the Liverpool Film Office, headed by Bridget Murray and her assistant Lynn Saunders, who were so helpful in helping me find locations and crew. At one point Bridget had fallen out with Sara and would only deal with myself or Justin. I asked Sara to concentrate on raising the money for the film and keep a budget. Justin was so supportive to me Whenever I felt down or about to give up he brought me back with the line:

"Dad you're going to finish this film and it's going to be good."

The casting was something I was looking forward to, as it is the most important part of the process. You cast the right people and the rest is easy. My main characters were Jack, the lead little boy, his grandad, Tom and three of Jack's friends, all aged between 7 and 10. There was also the part of a bully boy; he would be around 13 or 14. So we put an ad in the Liverpool Echo and rang up most of the schools around Liverpool. The

John McArdle

adult parts were a little easier because I knew who I wanted. I offered the grandad to veteran actor Tony Booth and Jack's mother to Nicola Stephenson. They both said yes. Now it was time to cast the kids and what a task that was. I wanted these actors to look like the characters I had written and pictured in my mind. I wanted them to be very natural and real, not stage school-trained. Justin and I would make appointments at the schools to audition the kids and later we would discuss any possibilities.

After about three weeks we had cast Jack's mates and the bully boy. Casting Jack was proving hard because I wanted it to be so right – after all, the film was about him. It was getting close to the actual filming and I still hadn't cast Jack. One evening after working on pre-production we had a casting session in the film office, and lots of young hopefuls arrived to audition for Jack. One particular kid that was auditioning was a bit too old for the character but I let him read anyway. After he had finished reading I thanked him and as he was leaving he said he had his younger brother with him, but he hadn't done any acting before, would it be alright if he came in to read? He wasn't on the list but I said I would see him anyway. the little lad came in and he looked exactly like the Jack I had in my mind. But we had to find out if he could act.

This kid was a natural and when he had finished reading I asked him a few questions about what he thought of the script. He very honestly replied that he had not read it and that he would when he got home. As soon as he left, I knew this was our Jack. Justin knew too; he had seen the look on my face. I asked Justin to phone this lad's mum and dad and tell him that their son has been offered the part of Jack in the short film *The Duke*. His name was Lee Gilbert.

I found out that it's a very stressful business making a film. Whether it's fifteen minutes long or an hour and a half you still have to prepare to the same degree. Everything has to be booked well in advance: the actors, the crew, the locations, the props, wardrobe, make up, special effects, equipment, catering, hotels, transport. It takes great organisation and thank God I had a wonderful team, especially my son Justin and Sara. Even though I didn't get on with her she was good at her job. I had an excellent crew; my Director of Photography was Bruce McGowan, an award winning DOP from the film *Letter to Brezhnev* and Martin Beresford as sound engineer.

We were getting near the filming date and we'd not yet raised any money. Even with actors and crew giving their services for free, it was still going to cost in the region of £25,000. Although I had been doing very well financially, there was no way that I could finance this film alone, after all I had to take three months out and that meant turning work down, which I did on a number of occasions. But for this film to go ahead we had to put in some of our own money. I was prepared to cut back on production costs and make the film on 16mm instead off 35mm and shoot the film in 4 days instead of 5. But Sara wanted the full effect and said she would put up some money if I was prepared to do the same. What could I do? It was my film. So I discussed it with Kathy and she gave it her blessing. She said after all the hard work that had been put into this film by everyone, I couldn't not go ahead.

So we would start shooting on September the 7th, 1998. The night before we started filming I was so nervous, more nervous that any first night of theatre. There was so much riding on this film, the money, the responsibility of finishing on time, as most of the crew were going onto other paid jobs in a few days. Justin, Sara and I went to the pub near our production company offices for a celebratory drink and met up with Colin McKeown. Colin was a producer that I had worked with on *Brookside* and was now a successful independent TV and film producer. I was telling him how nervous I was about tomorrow and he gave me the best advice for any first time director.

John McArdle

He said, "Tomorrow every head of department will want you to make a decision very quickly. The first assistant will want to rush you, the art director will want to know if you like the colour of the curtains, the makeup will want you to see the haircuts, the runner will ask you if you want a cup of tea and where the keys of the Volvo are. Do not be distracted by all that. Your focus is on the story and how you want it told by the camera. Never be rushed, after all you only have this day to get what you want on that camera. You just concentrate on your actor's performances, and how you want it to look onscreen. The rest can be left to your First Assistant Director. If this was the army you would be the captain, your first would be your Sergeant Major and the crew are your élite troops."

It was such good advice. I didn't sleep much that night, but I knew what I had to focus on for the shot.

The first scene of the day was the interior of a 1950s cinema. It was the scene when Jack goes to the cinema with his mother to see his first John Wayne film and realises that his grandad looks like John Wayne. The scene involved about 30 supporting artists and two main characters, Jack and his mum. I wanted a long tracking shot from the front of the cinema moving up to the two main characters, then remaining static for the rest of the scene. This may seem like a very simple scene, but it took three hours to film. Like I said earlier, I was so nervous about directing, but once I said *action*, then *cut* a few times, the nerves went and I was focused on what I wanted to do.

My crew were excellent. if I was unsure about anything, I would ask them and they would put me right. I made sure that every member of my family was in this film, as it was about my grandfather and he would have liked all his extended family involved. Kathy played the ticket lady at the cinema box office. She had to audition for the part like everyone else! I had to make sure she had a good enough Scouse accent, which she did, thank God or there might have been a few quiet days at home! Katie played the ice cream girl; Joe was one of the kids in the street. Kathy's sister Lynne, her husband John and their daughter Jessica were in the cinema scenes. My mother and I did a cameo coming out of the cinema, and even you were in it, Dad: Jack has a picture of his deceased father on his bedside table and it is a picture of you in army uniform when you were about 30. You got a big close up shot. Tony Booth was excellent as Jack's grandfather, Tom, and he was great with the kids. I struck up a good friendship with him during the making of *The Duke*, so much so he asked me to be the best man at his wedding to Stephanie Buckley. I shall tell you more about that later.

One of the highlights of the filming was the location of Jack and his grandfather's house. We actually used Wrights Terrace, the street where I had lived when the story was set; it hadn't changed that much, still a cobbled street and the houses were the same. It added a great feeling to the film and a personal touch for me. We managed to finish in the nick of time, as it poured with rain on the last day of filming. We moved the exterior shot to an indoor one and it worked out much better in the end. The important thing about making a film is your plan – you have to have a plan. You can change that plan anytime you like during the production, but your storyboard and shooting plan must be mapped out from the beginning. We had a great wrap party to thank everyone for their fantastic contribution, I couldn't have done it without them, and they were all invited to the premiere. I enjoyed directing *The Duke* enormously. It was a labour of love: stressful but a great moment in my life.

Next came the less stressful and more enjoyable post-production and editing. This is where you put all the pieces together to make the final product. This included titles and credits, editing, any special effects and of course, music. We needed an extra £5,000 to finish the film if we wanted to enter it for the festivals like Cannes etc. So we put out some begging letters to various companies to raise the money. We had no luck there, so it looked like we would not make the deadline for Cannes.

John McArdle

One night I was in the pub we used to go to when we were working on post-production. It was called The Vernon. It was just around the corner from the North West Film Office and the Liverpool Film Office, so you got a lot of media people in there. I got talking to Colin McKeown who was having a drink in there and told him of our plight. He came to the rescue straight away, saying that he would give us the £5,000 to finish our film in time. He didn't want repayment just a credit for his production company at the time, Lime Street Productions. So thank you once again, Colin. We manage to make it to the 1999 Cannes film festival.

Whilst Sara and Justin were sorting out the festivals and premiere venue, I was sitting in with the editor to piece the film together. And what an enjoyable time that was. The editor had already assembled a rough cut and he had done a marvellous job. He was giving his services for free and I was so lucky to have such good professional craftsmen and women helping me on this film. The editor Stephen Parry had a really good idea for the ending of the film. The last scene of the film is Jack and John Wayne riding off together down a terraced street in Liverpool. In the script I described them riding off into the Arizona sunset, but as Liverpool does not have desert sunsets, I thought it would be left on the page. Stephen said that if I wanted that ending it could be done, on computer with a product called Flame. Using this software would also erase TV aerials and burglar alarms, as there were not many about during the 50s.

Next I needed an original music score for the film and I was about to call on an old friend of mine, Stephen Warbeck, who I had worked with in the past. He was Musical Director on *You'll Never Walk Alone* which I did at the Everyman Theatre in 1985 and MD on *The Crucible* that I did in Sheffield in 1996. Since I had last worked with Stephen he had gone on to great heights in his career as a Musical Director and Composer, working continuously with the RSC and prestigious TV shows such as Prime Suspect 5, which I had worked on.

You Never Said Goodbye

I called Stephen and pitched my film to him. He was delighted with the story and agreed to write the music for it and he would waive the fee but I just had to pay his three musicians. Sara sent over the assembled format of the film to watch and I was to meet up with him to discuss my ideas on what I wanted for the mood of my film. Stephen suggested we do it sooner rather than later as he was working on a big project for a movie, but at this point he didn't tell me what it was. He asked me to come over and stay with him and his family for the a few days to work on the score. I joined Stephen and his family at their home in Highbury, London. We had a meal and then we went to a venue where he and his wife, and another friend of mine were performing with their wonderful band, The Kippers. When we got back from the gig, Stephen presented me with the score he had been working on, based on what I had discussed with him earlier. I wanted a mixture of Spaghetti Western and old Hollywood cowboy style but Stephen had come up with something much better than I could have imagined. It was perfect - moving, atmospheric and exciting.

The next day we set off for the studio to record the music for *The Duke*. On the way in we picked up two of the musicians who were going to work on it. One of them asked Stephen if Harvey Weinstein had been in touch regarding the music for *Shakespeare in Love*. He had never mentioned this to me before. Here he was working on my little short film, for no fee, and at the same time working on a big Hollywood Movie - what a guy!

We went into the studio to record the music and Sara met me there. It was so amazing Stephen had got the right style and mood of my film, we had it finished in a couple of takes He had given me a score for my film that exceeded my expectations. Stephen went on to win an Oscar for his music score for *Shakespeare in Love*. It couldn't have happened to a nicer or more talented man. Thank you once again, Stephen.

The film was now completed and was to have its first screening for cast and crew at the Odeon cinema on London Road, Liverpool, a

John McArdle

cinema that I have watched many a movie at. Little did I know that one day I would have my own film screened here. I was so nervous before the film started. The cinema was packed with the cast and crew and their families and friends – in total, about 400 people. I was so proud of this moment, seeing my name on screen in twenty foot letters as the Writer and Director of *The Duke*. I was also so proud of and thankful to all the people that had helped me make this film: cast, crew, family, friends and Sara. I admit I did not get on with Sarah; we clashed most of the time but she was a great Producer and helped to push the film on. She was responsible for getting it into some top festivals and getting lots of publicity.

The film was well received and it's next screening courtesy of Maureen Sinclair of BAFTA North was to be at The Royal Philharmonic, Liverpool. It was to be screened alongside *Hilary and Jackie*, a film by local writer Frank Cottrell Boyce and starring local actor David Morrissey and Angela Griffin.

My hard work was all done, so it was back to my day job as an actor. Kodak, who supplied the 35mm film for *The Duke*, invited us to the Cannes Film Festival to include us in their competition for emerging new European talent. It was so exciting to be in Cannes. If you remember the last time I was here I was just starting out as an actor and on my first holiday with Kathy and I'd said that the next time that I come here it would be by invitation for something that I had done in the film business. Well, that day had come and my film was to be screened at the world's most prestigious film festival. Being here was a dream come true, walking along the Cote d'Azur with its palm tree lined promenade and beautiful people. I had to pinch myself.

The film won the Best Short with Kodak for Emerging New European talent. The film went on to be screened at many film festivals including Venice, Edinburgh, Brisbane, Seattle, Palm Springs, Los Angeles Film

Institute, Sienna, Iran and BAFTA LA. It also won another award for Best Short Film at the Giffoni International Film Festival in Italy. The film was a story inspired by my grandfather and included my whole family, and I was so proud.

I had known Tony Booth prior to making *The Duke*. We used to meet at Labour Party functions and canvassing tours. During the making of the film we became much closer and as a result he asked me to be his Best Man at his forthcoming wedding. The wedding was to be held at the St Francis de Sales RC Church in Walton, Liverpool in 1998. Also attending was his daughter Cherie and the Prime Minister Tony Blair. The Blairs had rushed from the Labour Party Conference in Blackpool to be there. So as not to upstage the bride and groom the Blairs arrived half an hour early and waited in the church.

Tony's cousin, Father John Thompson made a bit of a gaffe. Because this was Tony's 5th wedding, Father John said during the wedding vows, "Do you, Anthony Booth take Stephanie Buckley to be your lawful wedded wife - again?"

Everyone in the congregation just fell about laughing. It was a great moment. I had to do a reading and Tony Blair had to do one after me. When we were back at the reception, Tony Booth took me to one side and said, "Your reading was better than the Prime Minister's, John."

I met the Prime Minister twice after that, once at Tony's 70th Birthday party and once at Number 10, when I was invited with a number of other actors, including Helen Worth of *Coronation Street* and Patrick Stewart, star of both stage and screen. I found Tony Blair easy enough to talk to and he was interested in what you had to say. I must say Cherie Blair was much harder work to talk to; she had none of her father's charm and warmth and I found her cold and unfriendly. I escorted their son, Ewan to a Liverpool v West Ham match at Anfield. He usually went with his grandfather Tony Booth, but he was unwell and asked me if I would like to go to the match and look after Ewan. This was a great opportunity for me, being a LFC supporter for most of my life and taking the PM's son with me.

Ewan was about 18 at the time. He had just started university and like all fresher students he got drunk and got up to mischief – a normal thing to do when you're young and it's your first time away from home. Poor Ewan though got bad press for doing what is expected of most young students. I found him to be modest and good company. After the match I took him down to the Players' Lounge to meet some of the players and get some autographs. He was too shy to ask for them himself, so he asked me if I would do the honours. A few of the players knew me from my *Brookside* days: Jamie Carragher and Stephen Gerrard being two of them. They didn't know Ewan was the PM's son and Ewan didn't really care if they knew or not – as I said, he was a modest young man. He got all their autographs and went home a happy lad.

I like many other Labour supporters voted for Blair in 1997, and I helped with many campaigns for the Labour party throughout the years. However, my support for Blair changed when he dragged us into the unnecessary Iraq War. Shortly after that war the Labour party asked me to make a promotional video for the upcoming election and asked me what my stance was on the Iraq war. When I told them I was against it they dropped me from the video and have never asked me to help them since.

Even though some interest was shown for me to direct other projects I decided it wasn't something I wanted to do. It wasn't that I didn't like doing it - there's nothing more satisfying than creating something from your vision and putting it altogether on a big screen - but I found it hard work and too stressful. I never slept and you were constantly thinking about the work all the time. It felt such a responsibility and it seemed to consume your life until the very last day of post-production. Maybe I'm lazy and don't want to put in all the hard work but I find it much easier to be in front of the camera!

My TV career was still prolific. Straight after finishing *The Duke* I went on to do a BBC series called *Born to Run*, written by Debbie Horsfield. It was a great script with a wonderful cast. I was to be playing opposite one of my favourite actresses, Billy Whitelaw. In fact the nineties was my busiest period working in TV and Film.

I had now reached the age you'd been when you left us, 48, and I felt like I had reached my final year. Ever since that day of your death I have constantly worried about having a heart attack and dying prematurely. When I was younger I thought that I would die before 48 so I lived life a little recklessly, then I had children and I wanted to be around for them, so I started to look after myself. I did more exercise, stopped smoking, and tried to eat healthily.

When I reached 50 I went to the doctors for a check-up and he said that I had high blood pressure and high cholesterol. The doctor told me my condition was mostly hereditary and that the only way to prevent a heart attack or stroke was to go on medication for the rest of my life. I left the surgery depressed and down because I felt that all the healthy eating and exercise was doing me no good. I had your genes, Dad, and I felt there was nothing I could do about it. But at least I had a choice - to take medication and hopefully live a long life. If these medicines were available in your time, Dad, you may have lived longer. Things have moved on so much since you were alive Dad and I'm thankful to be fit and healthy.

One particular job I enjoyed working on was *The Cazalets* by Elizabeth Jane Howard. I went up for the part of Tunbridge the chauffeur to the Cazalet family. I was to meet Verity Lambert and Joanna Lumley, the

John McArdle

producers, having already been approved by the director, Suri Krishnamma who I had worked with on *The Place of the Dead*. It was a lovely meeting with the two producers and found I had a similar upbringing to Joanna Lumley as she was also born into a military family and had travelled quite a lot when she was a child so we got on very well. On the drive home from the interview, my agent rang me and said they had offered me the job. Well that was quick – wish they were all like that!

It had a tremendous cast including Hugh Bonneville, Frederick Treves, Lesley Manville and Paul Rhys, a good friend of mine from *Gallowglass*. It was wonderful working on such a wonderful BBC costume drama. Frederick Treves was a great guy to work with, a little eccentric and funny but this actor had such a brilliant CV. He had been in lots of films and had done all the great spy thrillers of the 60s and 70s.

One day we were resting in our three way Winnebagos, long caravans with three separate compartments for the actors to sit in and wait to be called on set – a bit like cells really! It was a hot day so we left the doors of these rooms open to let in the fresh air and also to see who was around to talk to. I had just been for a cup of tea and was returning to my three way van. I was in costume so I was wearing my jodhpurs, shirtsleeves and braces.

As I was walking past Frederick's door, he shouted, "Tunbridge, can you fetch me a cup of tea? There's a good chap."

I stopped dead in my tracks.

"Sorry, are you talking to me Frederick?" I said.

"Yes I am as a matter of fact, tea please and quickly."

I didn't know if he was method acting or he was losing it, so I said, "I am not really Tonbridge, you know, I am John McArdle, an actor like yourself."

Fredrick put down his paper and said, "Sorry old chap, forgot about that."

In the end I did give him my cup and got myself another.

It was lovely working with him – we had such a laugh together. Also it was great to work with Paul Rhys again; he's such a wonderful actor and a great bloke. Paul is such a genuine person, never changes and is always glad to see you. He didn't care what anyone thought about him and was his own man. We were having a chat one day when this very rude and precocious 10year old girl kept interrupting our conversation. She was playing one of the children from the Manor House.

She kept butting in and saying things like, "So you're just playing the chauffeur, the one who drives us around, are you?"

Paul couldn't take any more. He turned to her and said, "And you're driving us mad, now go away!" (or words to that effect!)

The girl just turned and ran off to tell her chaperone. The rest of the cast and crew all had smiles on their faces as this little monster had had her comeuppance.

This was one of the reasons I'd left *Brookside*. Although I loved working there, it taught me such a lot and I will always to be grateful to it, I became an actor to play different characters, from all walks of life and different periods of history. It felt great to have the opportunity to be able to do that. When I was leaving *Brookside* Mal Young was the producer. In the five years I had been at Mersey Television, Mal had made his way up from standby props to Producer. He hadn't changed that much and rapid promotion didn't go to his head. Phil Redmond saw this in him and gave him the opportunity to succeed. When I approached Mal to tell him I was leaving he was very practical about it, he didn't try to stand in my way or beg me to stay. He said I was a versatile actor and he thought I was doing the right thing. He also said if things didn't work out I could always come back, but he didn't think that would happen.

It was six years after I had left that he asked me to be part of a new series he was producing for Channel 4 called *And the Beat Goes On*, set in Liverpool during the 60s Merseybeat era. It was eight one-hour episodes and followed two contrasting families through the music scene of that exciting period. It was whilst we were making this that he mentioned a future project he had in mind that he wanted me to be part of. I put this at the back of my mind as most projects you are offered never come to fruition. But this particular one did. Four years later, Mal, true to his word, and at this point Head of Drama for the BBC, rang me and asked if I was still interested in the idea he'd told me about. It was a police drama for the BBC set in Merseyside and he was offering me one of the main characters. This was a dream job, filmed less than an hour from where I lived, a great part with a good script and great pay. Of course I was interested, and after discussions with my agent and the BBC, I said yes.

We had a brilliant cast which was to be headed by Haydn Gwynne, as the superintendent. I was to play Inspector Jim Oulton, David Hargreaves as sergeant, Jonathan Kerrigan as Police Constable along with Michelle Holmes, Chris Walker, Eileen O'Brian and about four young newcomers. It was about the everyday lives of policemen and women serving in the North West of England. It followed their work and their home lives, their home lives being equally as dramatic as their police work. We had been filming for three weeks under the title *Silver Command* but Mal and the writer Chris Murray weren't really happy with this name. They wanted something that reflected the area it was set in. As it was set just outside Liverpool near Runcorn and Widnes in Merseyside, they came up with the title *Merseybeat*.

Mal called me into his office one day to discuss who would play my on-screen wife. Mal was good like this. He included you in the casting process sometimes and it makes sense. You would be working alongside this person for the next few years so it would be good if you got along with them as well as them being right for the part. Mal ran a few names by me and then asked did I have any ideas.

I said, "How about Kathy?"

"Kathy who?" replied Mal.

"Kathy Jamieson, my wife," I said.

Mal said, "Perfect – the chemistry must work if you've been married 17 years. Ask her to come in and discuss it with me, see if she's interested."

She was interested and she got the part playing my screen wife, Dawn Oulton. This was only the second time we had worked together in our twenty-year acting career. The first time was when I had joined her on a series she was a regular in, *How We Used to Live*, that time she couldn't keep a straight face because I was playing a posh doctor with hair parted in the middle and a very ill-fitting suit. But this time Kathy was to be a semi-regular and we had some difficult scenes to film later in the series. This series was different to other police dramas as nearly half of it concentrated on the private lives of the police, their domestic problems, money worries, love lives and so on – after all, they're only human like the rest of us. We had a great time filming, with a wonderful cast and a brilliant crew.

One day we were filming some scenes at the Oulton family home. Kathy and I would sit in a corner while they were setting up and go through our lines together and as we were really man and wife we were very familiar with one another. We would have a laugh and mess about until we were called on set. One of the makeup girls told us that one of the electricians thought we were having an affair. He didn't know that we were married in real life, as Kathy's Equity name is Jamieson, not McArdle so he thought we were up to no good. We told the makeup girl not to let him know the real situation, and we played up a bit being a bit more familiar with each other than you would normally be with a screen partner - the odd kiss, getting changed in the same room etc. This infuriated the electrician; he thought it was outrageous to flaunt our affair in front of the crew like this. I must say this is very unusual for a spark; they don't usually give a damn what you do. He must have had a moral conscience. We kept this up for about two weeks, and then we had to tell him - it was getting to the stage that he wouldn't look you in the eye or say hello. He did take it in good humour though when we told him. I think he was relieved.

We also had some great guest actors on Merseybeat: Kevin Wheatley, Duncan Preston, Paula Wilcox, John Henshaw and many more. Location filming was always good fun, you would be out there in your police cars and police uniforms and you noticed how the general public would react to you. Usually they gave way to you when driving in traffic and they would sometimes ask you for directions or advice.

One particular day we were filming in Liverpool city centre and all the makeup trucks and Winnebagos were parked up on some waste ground. I wasn't needed for a few hours so I walked around the back of the caravans into the street.

A bloke approached me; he stopped and said, "You're Billy Corkhill, aren't you?"
"Well I played him," I replied
He looked at me in my police uniform and said, "So you're a copper now are you? Always wondered what happened to you after Brookside." Then he walked off shaking his head.
Another day we were on our way to a location just outside the city centre, when we stopped at some traffic lights on Man Island, near the Pier Head. There were three rows of traffic at the lights and we were in the middle row. We were in a small people carrier, four of us already dressed in our police uniforms. Just in front to our left was a BMW 3 series car and adjacent to us on the left was a VW Golf. The lights were on red but the Golf started to ram the BMW, then we noticed that three cars back from the Golf was an Audi A4 convertible with a bunch of lads in it. One of the lads from the Audi jumped out and ran to the Golf. I looked out of the window and noticed he was hiding something in his hand – he was shielding whatever it was with his other hand. I thought *he's got a gun and we're about to witness a shooting.* This guy opened the driver's door to

the Golf and the driver got out and shouted to his girlfriend to lock the doors. Meanwhile the guy from the Audi punched the guy from the Golf twice in the stomach. When he drew back his fist I could see blood on the shirt of the Golf driver, he must have stabbed him, and he then ran like mad across the busy main road and into the city. His girlfriend was screaming in the car. The guy from the Audi then ran back to his car and sped off. Then the traffic lights changed to green and everyone but the BMW and Golf drove off including us. It all happened so fast, we told our driver to stop and see if the girl was ok, but while we were watching all this happen he had already phoned the police. We had no idea what it was all about. Was it a drug deal gone wrong? Was it someone with someone else's wife? Or was it just road rage? We didn't even find out what happened to the Golf driver: did he survive his knife attack? We never found out.

A few weeks before *Merseybeat* was to be launched, the BBC held a dinner to launch all the forthcoming programmes for the new season. It was held in Manchester and lots of the key people involved in the new programmes would be attending. It covered all aspects of BBC TV, Drama, Documentaries, Comedies and Sport. We were seated on tables with a mixture of guests and I was sitting on a table with Greg Dyke, Alex Ferguson, and some other TV executives. We all had place cards with our names on them. There was a little chit chat, then they started to show clips of what was coming up in the new season of programming. After a few clips of sport and comedies they showed a clip of *Merseybeat* and I was featured in it.

Alex Ferguson noticed it was me on screen. He turned to me and said, "So you're an actor then?"
I replied, "Yes, and what do you do?"
A wide smile spread across his face.
"And I bet you support Liverpool FC."
"Of course I do," I said.

John McArdle

I had a good conversation with him that evening and found him to be good company, a very funny and interesting man. I met up with him on a couple of occasions; one at a Labour Party rally, as he was an avid supporter of the party, and once at the BBC Sportsman of the Year dinner, where he introduced me to two other football legends, Nobby Stiles and Bobby Charlton.

This is My Life

Something was about to happen that I'd dreamt about and imagined many times but never thought would happen. The year was 2002. I got home from work at 'Merseybeat' after a very busy week. It was Friday night and I was looking forward to having a few drinks and relaxing with my family.

At about 8pm, I got a phone call from our production manager to say that I had to come into work on Sunday as the episode was running short. We needed a two-minute scene and I had to lead the scene. They said they were sorry but it had to be done. They emailed me the scene, which was set in the control room of the police station, with nearly every member of the cast involved, so I wasn't the only one who had to come in on their day off. I had most of the dialogue in the scene so I would have to stay in and learn it.

I got to work on Sunday at around 11am so it wasn't too early a start. As I said, the scene was set in the control room and the whole cast was in it, so it was going to be a long shoot. I felt good because I was on top of the scene and it was going very well apart from a couple of cast members forgetting their lines. We shot this scene from so many angles; I thought the director was really milking it. After about the eleventh take I was getting a bit cheesed off.

Chris Walker was forgetting his lines all the time, and I said, "Come on Chris, I want to get home."

We were in the middle of the twelfth take and it was going well, but there seemed to be some noise coming from behind me. I decided to ignore this: *if the director cuts then I will stop.* Then Chris dried again and started smiling and looking over my shoulder. I turned to see what he was looking at and to my surprise I saw Michael Aspel carrying a big red book. *Wow*, I thought, *He's come for Lesley Ash*. She was standing just in front of me (she had joined the cast after Haydn had left)

But no, he passed her and came to me and said the immortal words: "John McArdle – This is Your Life."

I couldn't believe it! Everyone started clapping and cheering and Michael Aspel told me that I would be whisked away somewhere nice until they were ready to film later on. In fact they had booked me a room at the V&A hotel in Manchester, next to Granada Studios where it was to be filmed. I had a lovely room with lots of food and drink and flowers. No alcohol though; they wanted me sober for the time being. I was being kept at the hotel so I would not see any of the guests arriving. It was a long wait but it was going to be worth it. I was so excited about this event, not nervous at all; I couldn't wait for it to begin. Kathy had got together a couple of shirts and suits for me to wear for the show. Kathy had kept this whole thing a secret from me for the past three months. She had had to liaise with the researchers and production staff on *This is Your Life* to plan who would be on the show, and she had to keep this from me all that time. She'd done a wonderful job because I never had a clue this was going to happen. She told me later that there were times that she'd nearly been caught; she would have to ring off many a time when I would walk in on her conversations with the researchers. She thought I might think she was having an affair! I had never suspected a thing.

I had been sitting on my own in this luxurious cell for about four hours waiting for them to start the show. At around 7pm they led me out of the hotel to a dressing room just off the studio we were to film in. The floor manager came to collect me to lead me onto the stage to start *This is Your Life*. I was standing in the wings waiting for my introduction, excited and feeling great. Michael Aspel made his introduction and I stepped out onto the stage. The studio was packed with friends and relatives and they gave me a fantastic welcome. Michael gave a short speech about my early life and showed some clips of the work I had done throughout my acting career. The first guest to come through the curtain was Kathy and she looked more beautiful than ever. My love for her grew even more. Then my lovely children Justin, Katie and Joseph came on. I was so proud of them, and so would you be, Dad.

On one side of the stage sat my close family and friends. Everywhere I looked I could see familiar faces and friends old and new. My mum was beaming with pride and so were my brothers and sisters. Then my old *Brookside* friends came on, so great to see them, and of course all the *Merseybeat* cast. The individuals that followed were so well chosen by Kathy, each person someone I liked and cared about, especially Sue Johnston, Tony Booth, John Henshaw, my old mate Seamus O'Neill and Kate Williams from Drama School. All great people, actors and good friends. What a privilege and pleasure to be able to share stories about my life not just with my friends and family but with a huge TV audience as well. It felt like wonderful recognition of my work and life.

The biggest surprise of the night was when my old mate Loz Yates turned up all the way from Australia. I hadn't seen him for 29 years and it was so great to see him; we relived our time in Mount Eden Prison. The last guest to come on was my old drama teacher from Northampton College of Further Education, Martin Banks – the man responsible for me becoming a professional actor. This evening was one of the most special moments of my life. I wish you could have been there, Dad.

After the show there was a big party, it was like being at a big wedding. The BBC did a wonderful job, and I thank them for it. After the party in the studio we all went back to the hotel and carried on the party until about 5am. I think everyone enjoyed themselves. I was to see Loz again two years later when I went back to Australia to film a Mini Series called 'Through Her Eyes' about the baby who was snatched and killed by Dingo's. Kathy and Joseph were able to join me for a couple of weeks as the Production Company paid for them to fly out. I stayed with Loz for a few days while I was out there and we're still in touch.

I continue to have a successful career doing the job I love, Dad, but I thought this was a fitting place to finish. This was a milestone in my career and was an opportunity to look back on my life and reflect on all that had happened since those childhood days in Liverpool with you and mum and on all the things you've missed. We all have things we look back on with sadness and regret but you can't change the past and so I choose to be an optimist and always hope that things will work out for the best. It's hard to know what you would have thought of it all or of the man I have become but I hope most of all that you would have been proud.

I know I didn't turn out to be a boxing champ or a pro footballer, but I did find what I was good at, and to be an actor has been a joy and a privilege for the past 35 years. Ever since that day at school when I stood on stage for my first time I knew this was for me, that this is where I feel at home. Even during the ten years I spent working on building sites and being a scaffolder, at the back of my mind I wanted to be an actor. Of course I have a lot of people to thank for my becoming one. Credit must go to Jasia for encouraging me to better myself educationally and therefore joining the college drama group, Martin Banks my drama tutor for giving me the confidence to go to drama school. The tutors at my drama school who saw the potential in me to become a professional actor, especially Kate Williams, Janet Nelson and Janis Balotis. Meeting my lovely wife Kathy, who believed in me from day one and gave me her utmost support throughout my career. Even though she is a brilliant actress herself she took a back seat to bring up our children, a sacrifice she has never regretted. My mother and my brothers and sisters who have given me their loyal support from the day I left drama school. And my loyal friends that have stuck with me through good and bad times. You would also be very proud of your grandchildren, Dad. Justin, the eldest, is a film producer in Australia. He got there through hard work, starting as a runner, at the age of 25 co-producing *The Duke* and going on to direct adverts and short films. He is now married to lovely Tamsin with two beautiful daughters Wilhelmina and Emmanuelle. Katie, who got into York University, is now an actress and has performed in many successful plays. Joe who is at Edinburgh University studying Religious Studies and English Literature, is also good actor and also found a talent for stand-up comedy. The only regret is that you are not here to see them for yourself, Dad, although your life has lived on through our

John McArdle

memories of you and your photos. You are mentioned almost every day by your family, and as the Bob Dylan song goes, *You are forever young.*

Your loving son,

John x

You Never Said Goodbye

Michael Aspel giving me the big red book

From the left my brothers Rory and Terry,
brother in law John and Andrea, Rory's partner.

John McArdle

From the left, my sisters, Sharon, Coleen, Tricia and Mum Edie.

Greeting my family on This is your life. Justin, Katie, Joseph and Kathy

Selective List of Principal Performances in Theatre, Film and Television

Theatre

Stirabout Theatre Company	Music and comedy sketches in English prisons	dir. Corrina Seeds	1980
Contact Theatre Manchester	Lulu, (Wedikinds)	dir. Richard Williams	
	Accidental Death of an Anarchist (Dario Fo)	dir. Peter Fieldson.	1981
Liverpool Everyman	Lennon	dir. Bob Eaton	
	Old King Cole	dir. Ken Campbell	1982
Chester Gateway Theatre	Wind in the Willows (Kenneth Grahame)	dir. Peter Fieldson	
	Macbeth (William Shakespeare)	dir. Philip Partridge	1983
Liverpool Everyman Theatre	Bouncers. (John Godber)	dir. Danny Hiller	1984
Bolton Octagon Theatre	Two (Jim Cartwright)	dir. Andy Hay	1989
Young Vic Theatre	Two (Jim Cartwright)	dir. Andy Hay	1990
Liverpool Playhouse	Raving Beauties (Dave Simpson)	dir. Bob Thompson	1993
The Crucible Theatre	The Crucible (Arthur Miller)	dir. Robert Delamere	1994
National Theatre Studio	The Arbor. (Andrea Dunbar)	dir. James Kerr	1996
Liverpool Playhouse	Our Country's Good (Timberlake Wertenbaker)	dir. Edward Dick	2007
Bolton Octagon Theatre	Oh, What a Lovely War (Charles Chilton/ Gerry Raffles)	dir. Mark Babych	2008
English Touring Company	Little Voice. (Jim Cartwright)	dir. Alexander Holt	2009
Empire Theatre Liverpool	One Night in Istanbul. (Nicky Allt)	dir.	2009
Bolton Octagon Theatre	Demolition Man. (Aelish Michael)	dir. David Thacker	2011
York Theatre Royal	Brassed Off. (Mark Herman/ Paul Allen)	dir. Damien Cruden	2014

John McArdle

Television

Coronation Street (Scouse Sammy)	dir. Bill Gilmore	Granada TV
Charlie (Shop Steward)	dir. Martin Campbell	Central TV
Fell Tiger (Reporter)	dir. Stephen Butcher	BBC 1
How we used to Live (Dr Wallace)	dir. Carol Wilkes	YTV
Frankie and Johnny (Phil Walsh)	dir. Martin Campbell	Granada
Brookside (Billy Corkhill)	dir. Various	Mersey TV
Underbelly (Preston)	dir. Nick Renton	BBC 2
Thacker (Martin Strickland)	dir. Richard Spence	Screen 2 BBC
Gallowglass (Paul Garnett)	dir. Tim Fywell	BBC1
Skallagrigg (Dylke)	dir. Richard Spence	BBC2
Bambino Mio (Harry)	dir. Edward Bennett	BBC Screen1
The Chief (DC Corbyn)	dir. AJ Quinn	Anglia TV
Firm Friends 1&2 (Peter Cresswell)	dir. David Hayman/Sara Harding	Zenith
Finney (Louis Souter)	dir. David Hayman	Zenith
Seaforth (Fred Spence)	dir. Peter Smith/Stuart Burge	Initial
Cracker 2 (Carter)	dir. Jean Stewart	Granada
Rich Deceiver (Malc Freeman)	dir. Gurinder Chadha	BBC Screen
Wycliffe (James Kerr)	dir. Patric Lau	HTV
Kavanagh QC (Simon Lloyd)	dir. Charles Beeson	Central TV
In the Place of the Dead (Major Ron)	dir. Suri Krishannama	LWT
And the Beat Goes On (Charlie Woods)	dir. Chris Bernard/Various	Mersey TV
Prime Suspect 5 (DCS Ballinger)	dir. Phil Davis	Granada
Throwaways (Spinder)	dir. Kim Flitcroft	Zenith North
Playing the Field (Graham)	dir. Adrian laughland	Tiger Aspect
Out of Hours (Dr Daniel Lang)	dir. Douglas McKinnon	Monogram BBC
City Central (Michael Dennison)	dir. Tim Leandro	BBC 1
Holby City (Kenny)	dir. James Howes	BBC 1
Metropolis (Steve)	dir. Glen Wilhide	Granada
Where the Heart Is (Eddie)	dir. David Thacker	United Film & TV
Peak Practice (Clive Richards)	dir. Terry McDonough	Carlton TV
In Defence (DCI Brian Walsh)	dir. Roy Battersby	ITV
My Fragile Heart (Roy)	dir. Gavin Miller	Tiger Aspect

The Cazalet Chronicles (Tonbridge)	dir. Suri Krishanamma	BBC2
Gifted (Steve)	dir. Douglas McKinnon	Rolem Productions
Dalziel and Pascoe (Matthew Davis)	dir. David Wheatley	BBC 1
Merseybeat Series 1, 2 &3 (Jim Oulton)	dir. Andy Hay/Various	BBC 1
The Bingo Club	dir. Sarah Lancashire	BBC 1
Blue Murder	dir. Suri Krishanamma	LWT
Casualty/ Holby Xmas special (Frank Morgan)	dir. Michael Offer	BBC 1
Heartbeat (Terry Tiniswood)	dir. Graham Harper	YTV
The Bill (Len Perkins)	dir. Nicholas Laughland	Talkback Thames
(Phil Lane)	dir. Chris Clough	
(Geoff McKane)	dir. Ed Fraiman	
(Commander Ian Barratt)	dir. David Holroyd/Various	
Foyles War (Stan Davis)	dir. Gavin Miller	Bentley Productions
Munich Air Crash (CHARACTER)	dir. Matthew Wortman	BBC2
All the Small Things (Jimmy)	dir. Cilla Ware/Metin Huseyin	BBC1
Mobile (Paul Perry)	dir. Stuart Orme	Granada TV
Waking the Dead (Murray Stuart)	dir. Andy Hay	BBC1
Casualty (Alun Jones)	dir.	BBC1
Waterloo Road (Oliver Mead)	dir. Various	BBC1
Law and Order UK (Dan Callaghan)	dir. Robbie del Maestro	ITV
The Case (Gordon McAllister)	dir. Sean Glyn/Paul Murphy	BBC1
Doctors 4 eps	dir. Adrian Bean/Various	BBC1
Holby City (Various) 4 eps	dir. Various	BBC1
True Crimes (Bill Jones)	dir. Various	ITV
New Tricks (Jim Marshall)	dir. Andy Hay	BBC1

Films

Janice Beard 45 WPM (Pyesek)	dir. Clare Kilner	Dacota Films
Function at the Junction (Richie Lance)	dir. Justin McArdle	

John McArdle

Rough Aunty (Donald)	dir. Jim Doyle	BBG Pictures
There's Only One Jimmy Grimble (Sniveller)	dir. John Hay	Impact Film
Through My Eyes (Peter McCauley)	dir. Di Drew	Network 7 Australia
Come Here Today (Father)	dir. Simon Aboud	Smudge Films
Love Tomorrow (Henry)	dir. Chris Moon	Delliah Films/Laluna Films
Friends of Money (Mr Eklund)	dir. Adam Lee Hamilton, Andrew London	CPYL Films
The Rochdale Pioneers (Dr Dunlop)	dir. Adam Lee Hamilton, John Montegrande	CPYL Films

Performed in numerous plays for Radio 4 including *Clockwork Orange* by Anthony Burgess and *The Spire* by William Golding.

Directing

Last Night Another Soldier	Stage play	Chester Gateway Theatre
The Duke	Film	Blue Feather Films

Awards and Accreditation

Winner of Best Actor (Merseybeat) Royal Television Society, 2002
Member of BAFTA
Listed in Debrett's *People of Today*
Winner of Canne Kodak new film maker
Winner Giffonni film festival, best childrens short film.

About the Author

Born in Liverpool to an army family, John McArdle was educated both in England and abroad. He left school at age fifteen to work at unskilled jobs and later returned to complete his education as an adult in order to be admitted to drama school.

McArdle earned a diploma in speech and drama before embarking on a successful thirty-year career in acting, for which he received an award for "best actor" from the Royal Television Society in 2002. He also wrote and directed a short film about his grandfather, which was screened at the Egyptian Theatre in Los Angeles and won awards at the Cannes Film Festival and the Giffoni Film Festival in Italy.

McArdle lives in northwest England with his wife and two children. He also has another son from a previous marriage.

CPSIA information can be obtained
at www.ICGtesting.com
Printed in the USA
LVHW081347311220
675526LV00014B/387